"As women, we get to hold life, we hold the universe inside."

—Jodie Rodenbaugh,
Founder of The School of Love Genius,
Master of Emotional Intellect

"You're never too young or too old to reinvent yourself. But you're not even reinventing yourself, you're just building and growing. As humans, we are not stagnant, we're always changing. So why not in career?"

—Eve Overland,
Celebrity Personal Trainer,
fit52 App Collaborator

"When a woman steps into her full power, just like that, the game changes"

—Erica Carrico,
International Coach of the Year 2020,
Award-Winning Money & Marketing Coach *Forbes*,
New York Times, Yahoo Finance

Come SWEAT or SILT

Come SWEAT or SILT

A GUIDE FOR
FEMALE ENTREPRENEURS
WITH GRIT

CALLIE KATZ

Sweat or Silt- *A Guide for the Female Entrepreneur*

Copyright © 2023 Callie Katz

StoryLauncher™ is a trademark registered in the United States Patent and Trademark Office.

All rights reserved.

No part of this book may be reproduced, stored in a retrieval system, or transmitted in any form or by any means—electronic, mechanical, photocopying, recording, or otherwise—without the prior written permission of the copyright holder. The only exception is by a reviewer, who may quote short excerpts in a review with appropriate citations.

Book cover design by StoryLauncher.com
Book interior design by StoryLauncher.com
Editing by Story Launcher www.StoryLauncher. com
Author's books are available for order through Amazon.com

Visit my website: www.luxe-lush.com

First printing: October 2023

Published by Story Launcher™

ISBN-13: 978-1-951451-13-4
ISBN-13: 978-1-951451-14-1
ISBN-13: 978-1-951451-12-7

Printed in the United States of America

The contents of this book, such as text, images, and other material contained in the Content are for entertainment purposes only.

For Papa: I can't wait for you to read it. Grandma, I will never forget the moment when you told me you thought I was bored and I should write this book. I know you both are in heaven raising a glass. We miss you dearly.

And to my Un-re-lent-ing Strength team…
for all of you who have been in my corner, GOD + Universe,
as I stepped into the unknown.

"The World Needs Who You Were Made to Be."

—Joanna Gaines

TABLE OF CONTENTS

Thank you in advance for your Amazon Review

Introduction	1
Right On Time	7
Build Your Own Damn Ladder	21
Gut Check	33
Closing The Gap	47
Powerhouse Partnerships	59
One Gutsy Mama!	73
Come Sweat Or Silt	89
Training For Life	99
Allergic To Perfect	113
Smoke And Mirrors	125
Breaking The Barrier	141
Drive	149
Turning The Pages	165
Beyond the Sidelines	179
Acknowledgments	183
Redefining Your Resources	187

INTRODUCTION

"In that water thick with silt I discovered that if you laid out face down and kicked your feet very fast when you came up for air you had moved forward, and I suddenly knew what swimming was about."

—George E. Spear

When I read this passage written by my grandfather, I suddenly knew what my journey was. Life is going to surround us with as much silt as we allow. There will always be silt. Silt is what gets caught up under your feet just when you think you can take another step forward. Silt is what attempts to hold you down and makes you feel stuck. However, if you choose wisely, and kick your feet fast enough, you can swim forward and out of the silt.

We all have a choice. Whether we choose to sink or swim, come sweat or silt, we get to choose every damned time.

Because of my grandfather's published piece, I sit here writing this to all of you. Coincidentally, I am in the silt as I complete this book. I feel pain, I have questions, I am trying to come up for air, and yet, I must keep kicking. I not only made a promise to myself and my heavenly grandfather, but to all of you as well. That there would be a published piece that pulled back the facade of what it takes to be a female entre-preneur and the trials and tribulations that one may go through when she decides that playing small is no longer an option! There is something to be said about our raw realities when we choose to be a part of this tribe. And, no matter where you are in this journey, whether you are knee-deep, just beginning, or hitting the jackpot, you know that it comes with a price. As much as we think we know how the bank of life works, there are often withdrawals made that we didn't ask for.

We didn't ask for our families to be murdered. We didn't ask for our spouse to be injected with anesthesia into the wrong artery. We didn't ask to be part of an abusive marriage. We didn't ask for personal tragedies that would shake our faith. We didn't ask for our bodies to break down on us. And we didn't ask to be overqualified for a job, only to end up broke. The one thing we did ask for—came from within. We asked ourselves…to not give up. No matter the punches we took.

These stories are testaments to the women who have moved mountains. To the women that have experienced the hard hike, and though it may be messy at times (okay, a lot of messy, they've continued to dig their heels in the ground walking the road less traveled. These women are the definition of 'True Grit.' They have defined the role of the female entrepreneur in more ways than *Google* will ever show you.

Over the years, I have come face-to-face with female entrepreneurs in many facets of business. And as I began connecting the dots, I saw them forming two very clear categories. One group of women wanted to just "check the box;" their businesses were fun and filled a space for the time being, even if it didn't succeed, it didn't have to-because plan B was already an option. In the other group of women, I saw that it *meant* something. There was this burning desire, this steadfast glimmer of hope, because what they had been taught or who they had been coached by told them it was possible.

This was the group I was attracted to and wanted to be a part of! This community of like-minded women were a part of something bigger than the eye could see. They were all fully owning the fact they were capable of growing past mere average expectations.

Here's the hard truth: not everyone sees it this way. Not everyone is pre-conditioned to push themselves outside of their comfort zone. Not everyone has grown up in an environment where it was *okay* to go for the job or career that is outside the norm —or different than their family's standards. It is not easy to walk outside the line.

Sadly, it can also be the very thing that holds us back from living a life of limitless luxury, what I call our "Champagne Dreams." Our Champagne Dreams allow us to live life and thrive on our own terms. They enable us to serve and teach others what we preach. It means we go after what we want, when we want, respecting others and their decisions along the way—even if it doesn't match our personal goals. It means we play with the scary as fuck *yeses*, even when we don't know how to cross the damn bridge. Choosing to become a female entrepreneur does not give you an absolute *yes* to your future. However, you *do* get to choose whether that *yes* means enough: whether it's sought after or gets pushed to the side. You make it happen.

How many of you have started something, only to find yourselves not finishing? I'll go ahead and begin this round of hands up! We all do it, and we are not alone. YOU are not alone. It doesn't mean we all failed, though. In fact: just the opposite. You will learn in the chapters ahead that the non-finishers walked away with valuable learning experiences. Walking away taught us what we didn't want. If it *meant* more, wouldn't we have stayed? Wouldn't we have fought a little harder?

It's only been over the last two years that I have come to realize that I was serving the wrong group of women. I was falling trap to their victimization and negativity, and my emotions felt out of whack. On the flip side, I was also surrounding myself with women that I admired and wanted to be mentored by. These women were go-getters. They made things happen for themselves. They were living out their own version of "Champagne Dreams."

I had to ask myself a hard question. Why wasn't I there as well? Why wasn't I just as deserving as the next woman in line? I had worked tirelessly for the last twenty years—building brands, working my ass off to transform my life and environment—and yet, I was still falling into hard times.

Once I dove deeper, I recovered the answer. It was because I was allowing others to determine my worth. Sound familiar?

I had to let go. I had held onto the end of the rope for way too long. A rope that no longer served me. It was not going to help me climb to the top of the kind of ladder I wanted to build for myself and my family, and it was time to set myself free. I had spent my entire life betting on myself in more ways than one. So, why was it different now?

Fast-forward to today and I'm building the first rungs on my new ladder. My luxury, public relations agency, Luxe + Lush, a partnership with a global proactive wellness company that helps our bodies through a path of of financial, physical, and spiritual wellness. . I don't have to work with someone based on operation politics. I don't have to work with someone that doesn't respect my time. Truth be told, I finally feel like I'm headed in the right direction, and damn, it feels good.

My ideal client is a female entrepreneur who is ready and willing to invest in herself. She's someone that could easily have a multi-million-dollar business but needs someone to show her how. She values coaching and is enthusiastically ready to learn from women that have achieved similar goals. She enjoys the luxuries that come with success (travel, self-care, vacation homes, high-end fashion) but she isn't afraid to work hard to attain the lifestyle she wants. She has Champagne Dreams.

I delight in moments full of gratitude and joy where champagne is well deserved! Nothing excites me more than watching self-made entrepreneurs spray that baby open! Truth be told, I've been known to spray a bottle or two!

When I work with fellow authors and entrepreneurs, there is something powerful about connection in elite partnerships. It makes everyone feel as though they've made it! And yet, we've all walked down the muddy road together. Even in my celeb-rity partnerships, everyone has a story to share.

That's why I've included stories of purpose and power in the following pages! To show you all what is possible beyond circumstances. I have personally known some of these women for years, and the others I feel were divinely connected at just the right moment. As collaborator Amber McCue would say, *"You are always right on time!"* She is right. When you get good at listening to the quiet voice inside your head, your fears dwindle as you know that what you need will always show up. More importantly, we need to take care of ourselves. To be a female entrepreneur is no easy feat. Our bodies will always keep score. My new friends, Eve Overland and Cara Clark, will illustrate that in their chapters ahead.

Have unshakeable faith in yourself. Not everyone is built to be a part of this tribe. You were given this gift by a higher power. I firmly believe that. Whether you are ready to jumpstart your business, are in search of investors, or are looking for the right team of coaches to help make your childhood dreams a reality, we've got you!

Come Sweat or Silt helps you build a profitable sustaining business. Using interviews and stories from some of the most well-known online coaches, authors, and wealth management teachers ensures that this book is a much-needed tool in the industry of personal development and business growth. *Come Sweat or Silt*, fills the gap beyond just the single coaching package or standard day planner—it is a roadmap of creation, True Grit, and unlimited success for those who are ready for it.

If you are reading this, I don't have enough words to tell you what this means to me. You are all helping fulfill a childhood dream of mine. And although I ventured off the path a time or two, I'm here now. It wasn't because I got lost, it was because I wondered what else was out there waiting for me. I wasn't going to settle, nor should you. Every woman has the ability and magic within her to achieve the dreams she's always wanted. With the right tools and knowledge, anything is possible. We are unrelenting leaders, paving the way to greatness for other female entrepreneurs so that they can also write their own rules and inspire others to fol-low. Make room for the next round of CEOs making waves in their industry—there's always room at the table.

Our time here is borrowed. What will you do with it?

RIGHT ON TIME

Meet Amber McCue, Business coach via *AMBERMCCUE.COM*, Co-Founder of Three Boudoir, Author + Speaker.

Lover of green juice and pizza let's get to know this modern CEO! She grew her side hustle into a $1M company, and today, her personal brand, Amber McCue, is well on its way to impacting 1 million business owners by partnering with entrepreneurs who are seeking to create a better life and business altogether.

Best of all, this gal's got strategy sessions for days and is well known for her annual Planathon events! As a former client, I know firsthand why Amber plus her team are all about hard work plus sweet success rewarded. Trust me, you might want to tuck this one into your back pocket, ladies!

CK: I've always known you were the real deal. Recap your journey for our readers!

AM: *It's interesting when I think about my journey long before I started my businesses. It started in college. I was a single mom and was pretty set. My daughter went to school with me, and I was not going to change my plans because of my life's circumstances. She was the perfect daughter to have in college—she was calm and chill. She would sit next to me while I was doing my homework and it ended up being a great experience for me. I hope she would say the same. She has some foggy, retold story memories!*

I got a job that I loved, and I realized I had a passion for small business. So even though I was doing something I really loved, I knew there was something different out there. I wanted to create freedom and flexibility. My husband was looking at a different career path, and we didn't know what was going to happen.

I decided I needed to step into running my own business. There were a lot of attempts that didn't work out, but it was really when I was in my MBA program that I began testing the waters. My first business is one I co-founded called Three Boudoirs. We began small with our first model and client, and then people started to notice as we grew larger organically. My business partner and I realized that we were doing something special. I had thought I was going to go down the life coaching path because I really love those one-on-one conversations that you have with people, but I kept getting drawn back to business. I loved focusing on business strategy, consulting, and growth. That was the role I played more in our photography business. I started out as a photographer and loved our mission, but I was not the best person to stay in that role. We began bringing on more photographers and I was able to focus on the business side more. Fast forward to today, I am now running two businesses; my consulting business, Amber McCue, and the photography business, Three Boudoir, that now operates in 18 cities across the United States. It is just unbelievable when you think you have a vision, an inkling, or a nudge, and when you just keep following it, even with the failures, what can happen.

CK: What were some examples of the failed attempts? I know we have all been there at one point or another.

AM: *I can't even name all the network marketing or direct sales companies I tried. For me, I wanted it to be 'The One.' It was really going to work that time. Another business I pursued was a personal concierge service (I still have the marketing materials). I wasn't focused or invested in it enough. So, just to name a couple….*

I think it's important to explore each idea because every time you learn something, and you get closer to the 'real deal.'

As you first began these businesses, what were some of the roadblocks you came upon? The moments you felt like you were crashing and then found yourself saying that this wasn't going to work.

One distinct moment I have was when my business partner and I were doing a photo shoot. I was the photographer, and she was the stylist at the time. We set our photo shoots up so there were always two people. One to really focus on the photography aspects, and then there was technical (making sure every strand of hair was in place, straps were in place, etc.). I was in the middle of the shoot thinking, what am I doing? I can't do this forever. I need to be doing something different. We need to run this business different. So, I texted my husband (or so I thought), telling him that this was not going to work, but instead, I texted my business partner. When she received the text, she said, "let's talk." That opened a very awkward moment as I was melting on the inside, so distracted that I had texted the wrong person, yet it was that very heartfelt, raw message that opened the opportunity for me to step back into a strategy role, being the visionary and elevating as the CEO.

The fact that she was open to that and supportive really prevented it from being a break of the business—and that's how I knew we were in it for the long haul. I could have sent that message to her intentionally and it would have been fine, but at the time, I thought it was a BIG mistake. It sent us down the path to grow and expand.

What feels like those breaking points is the breakdown before the breakthrough.

I call this, "flipping the pancake!" I learned that from a team at Zappos in the book, Delivering Happiness, the Zappos extension, and I learned that one side of the pancake may be burning; if you flip it over, there's still something to be learned and created.

Part of our role as business owners and founders is flipping pancakes!

We are professional pancake flippers! Things are going to come up, but there is something on the other side of that burnt pancake we can learn from and that was one of those moments.

Since you are a mother and CEO, you can take that into your household as well!

Everything! It's a life perspective. I know this isn't going well but flip the pancake! We can make something from this, or do we need to throw this one in the garbage? There's a lot we can do with it; you're so right.

Love it. Taking that model home to your family, how do you explain to mothers who are working?

I've been home working since Audrey was born. It's been 10 years, both full-time and part-time. Lily, my oldest daughter, who is now in college, was a baby. I've always been doing something from home, and we're just going to do this together. I have pictures where Lily is sitting to the left of me doing something, I'm in the middle, and then Audrey, who was two at the time (she's my middle), is sitting next to us playing on the computer. It's about bringing them into the process. That includes letting us get some work done together, or it includes I've got something really big that I'm working on right now and this is going to be a priority for the next six weeks, so at the end we will all celebrate! When I had big events or when I was working really hard on something, we would see it as a payoff for the family in the end. We may be focused and intentional and prioritizing that for a minute, but there's a payoff for everyone.

I love that it's a reward system for the family! By bringing the entire family into it, they know that Mom's working, and they see that Mom is in it for us and helping to create our lifestyle.

It's so true. When everything's virtual, it's hard to see the tangible actions from that. Even our youngest daughter, Harper—we lived in Ethiopia for two years and there it's an all-cash model. There were no credit cards used. When we got back to the United States due to the pandemic, we started using cards, ordering online again. She told us that we didn't have any real money, and could we call Grandma? She wanted to buy something but thought we didn't have anything that was real. I was like, what are you talking about? This is real, I'm working with clients, I'm working in the business; this is how we make money. She said, 'No,' that 'our money only works on Amazon!'

(LAUGHS). So, when we can bring them into those conversations, it becomes more real and works for everyone.

Here's to Amazon, everyone!

She also stated at a restaurant when we were paying and she hadn't seen money in a while, that our credit cards were not money. Because she saw real money in Ethiopia for so long, now we had to explain how our credit/debit cards worked. It was mind blowing!

With Three Boudoir, how did you all set up the structure to be operated in 18 states?

One at a time. When we first started the photography business, we were working from home, but also doing photo shoots at home. My family would leave during those times on the weekends so we could do the shoots. We operated the photography business part time as side hustles for three years as we still had full-time jobs. The first year we hit $80k in revenue still working part-time! We then expanded into neighboring cities. My partner and I learned we didn't have to do it all. We trained our first photographer and our shoot stylist at my home. Then, we had another photographer working in D.C., and it was one city at a time. Philadelphia was next, so we just started looking rationally and logically on how we could do this with a bit of ease, not growing too fast and really pacing ourselves in order to manage everything. We did that slowly for about ten years until we got into six cities. We moved like molasses! In 2020, when we had to shut down our business for four months because we couldn't see people in person, we realized 'let's take this time to add cities. Let's market and let people know when we open back up, we're going to be ready for you so book your photoshoot!' We opened in 10 more cities after that four-month shut down! It was amazing. We trained people virtually, we hired, we were really betting on ourselves. We had been laying the foundation for 10 years and expanded into 16 cities! In 2021, we added 10 more cities. Since then, we've slowed down a bit since there is a lot to focus on. We are managing teams and shoot schedules. We're back to pacing ourselves and our desire to serve more women and engage more women in this experience. It's back to the *balance. It's weird how something like a four-month shut down (again, flipping the pancake), arrives an opportunity.*

There's a word a coach of mine uses called the "bless-on." Most people during that time panicked, shut down, or lost money. It either taught you something, or you just froze in those months. You can always look at it from a different lens. Personally, for me, it was a blessing. I didn't realize how worn down I was and how I needed to create a new structure. I enjoyed it. It gave me a clear vision of what my next steps were, as you all took that time to build and expand your business, ensuring that you would profit once things let up. You didn't have to start from scratch.

Exactly. It is so true. I love that framing. It was truly a blessing totally disguised at the time because we didn't know. This is trusting and stepping into the unknown and into those right-on-time moments. You've got a nudge, you're hearing a voice, follow it. Because exactly what you need to do to take the next steps will present itself. Sometimes, I may have a vision that is not super clear, but it doesn't have to be. What needs to be clear is your next step and then the next. Right on time, you are going to arrive.

What made you branch out and create Amber McCue, LLC? You had this successful photography business and could have stayed solely with that. Was there something else pulling at you saying, 'I need more creativity?'

I knew as we started the Three Boudoir, I still had a passion for business that wasn't yet fulfilled. I had explored the business coaching + consulting realm after I had Audrey. Someone had said to me, 'Don't you wish you could just clone yourself?' This is what we were doing in the photography business, and what I had done in corporate—building structures and systems, supporting leaders, and hiring. I thought I could help people clone themselves. This is what I wanted to do and was doing in other areas of my life. I was seeing myself loving the business strategy, creating the vision, and determining how we could serve more women in the photography business. So, I pulled those interests into consulting. They were happening parallel to each other, but one was the mirror for the other.

You actually have a How to Clone Yourself program!

EXACTLY! We use that to build systems and to hire. We have 40 women in the photography business and share the methodology with our clients.

What is next for Amber McCue, LLC?

At Amber McCue LLC currently, our business model has evolved, and we work with entrepreneurs and modern CEOs who want to create their freedom business. We're going to formalize that more. How can we support more women by stepping into their modern CEO role as they are building their business?

I feel like you are a natural visionary. Were you like that 20 years ago?

Yes. I didn't see the role of visionary. I've always partnered with leaders my entire career. Even in corporate, I really supported where the business unit or lead could take a load off. Where their paths were and how I could help. That led to me playing the execution role: 'How do we make this happen?' How we implemented the strategies was a challenge for me; growing the business, I could see it and I could implement it, but at some point, I couldn't do both anymore.

Running a small business, you are in the weeds.

All of us on a team are in the weeds. I needed a partner in my business to help implement so I could continue to pull that vision forward. I always knew I was going to create something someday; I just didn't know what it was. All those failed attempts we spoke about just led me to those right-on-time moments.

What would you tell somebody that is just starting to create their brand and are in the trenches? They feel like they are at a breaking point and can't do it all. What position would you recommend they hire first?

I don't point to a specific position because we all have different strengths. We all have things that we're ignoring that might be revenue generating for us. Or there are those things we really excel at. For example, I'm good with seeing a growth plan and our financials, as I have an HR background. Those are things I stayed in the weeds on.

If you look at your organization chart and you are one person right now, you fill all the roles. At some point, something is going to fall behind; it could be bookkeeping. You have to fire you in that role.

Go back to the chart and see where you need to be fired, where you're not meeting the expectations for that role anymore or not operating in a place that is best for you.

Starting to break it down personally is the only way to go.

LOVE IT. You have an HR background and could have stayed there but chose to delegate instead. We tend to think that because we have the background, 'I can do this, I'm good enough,' but sometimes that's not always the best fit for your business.

Even those things that we are good at. A friend of mine, Lewis Schiff, wrote a book called Business Brilliant. He researched the differences between self-made millionaires and billionaires, and those who stay in the middle class. I may not be going for the billions, but the shift in thinking how we operate from running a business and the money mindset perspective was huge for me. It's someone in the middle class that stays in the DIY mindset of 'I'm going to do everything myself,' and it's the self-made millionaires and billionaires that have this mindset of 'if there is someone that could do this better than me…' That's what I started asking myself. To keep doing something excellent, you have to get someone to help you! That shift that Lewis shared in the book and the research he did was profound for me! There is someone better. It doesn't mean I'm bad, it doesn't mean I'm failing.

Let's leverage the collective brilliance of people that are doing great things and how can we come together to create even more great things?

Is there anyone that you look up to, or if you could get mentored, by who would that be?

That's a really good question. I've had mentors since the very beginning of running my business. I look for expertise in areas that are off set to mine. Sarah Blakely would be fun—LOVE her vibe! Give me Oprah all day! I heard Tony Robbins speak at an

Oprah event live, and he shared that you don't want someone to mentor you that is a bazillion steps ahead because it's so far out there. I look at Sarah Blakely and I would learn a lot; she's doing something completely different with a different business model. So, I look for people who are closer to what I am doing and specifically speak to gaps I may have.

I feel like I have a coach for every area of my life!

Yes! I'm working with James Wedmore and Shenee Howard from HeyShenee.com. They each have different perspectives, viewpoints, ways of marketing—we elevate when we get those different perspectives.

I firmly believe that no matter what level you are at, you should always find a mentor/coach to help you become greater than you already are.

I could not agree more. I think it's also good when you know them and they know you, as I have known James and Shenee a long time, to build and maintain those relationships. It's also good to reach out to new people and gain new perspectives that can be valuable as well.

For sure. I know you have favorite quotes and mantras that you live by, but what is one that holds true to the heart when you experience those tougher days?

In those tough moments, I always go back to RIGHT ON TIME. That mantra of living life right on time has been powerful for me.

It's impossible to be late for your destiny.

It could also be received as, 'don't worry, it's all going to work out and you don't have to take action,' BUT YOU DO! Right on time is about taking action every step of the way, with every calling and every nudge. I've lived my life that way for as long as I can remember. It was even more pivotal when I started working with clients and they were late or feeling pressured, and I would say, 'You are right on time.' It's about taking off that pressure and giving ourselves the freedom to step forward. There's so much pressure to hustle, to get ahead and to compete.

There was one year we were scheduled to move to the Congo. We were in a temporary apartment, and everything was already packed. The truck had left our place, my husband calls and says we're not moving. I said, "We already moved.' He said, "Change of plans, we're not moving yet." I wasn't sure what was going on. Something had happened with work. We didn't know when we were going to end up moving so we AirBnB hopped until then. Fifteen moves later, we landed in Ethiopia! Every step of the way I had asked for right-on-time moments. The blessings were unfolding right on time. We were supposed to be in Ethiopia, not the Congo. It never would have unfolded or happened that way had we not rolled with it.

Say yes to whatever is unfolding.

If you could tell a younger Amber how to conquer this path of being an entrepreneur, knowing your journey and the experiences, what would you tell her?

I would tell her that you got this! To keep going. There were so many times where I doubted, questioned, or wondered, 'Will this ever work?' Some things didn't work, but the right things did. Keep stepping forward, ask questions, and experimenting.

I tell that to my clients in general, 'You got this!' I think we learn so much about ourselves when we look back and see what we have conquered, yet sometimes the self-doubt still creeps up.

We have to let all of that go.

Is there a business bucket list for you? Is there something in your business that you have yet to check the box on?

The idea of sharing a mission on a stage in the likes of Oprah and Super Soul Sunday. With someone that has a platform that is aligned from the soul and spirit. That mission is elevating women. In both of my businesses, that's what I do. Not even in just women necessarily. It's bringing the work of femininity and immersing that through more. That would be something. We were recently recognized by Forbes *in their Next 1000. When people pull that out, that's those right-on-time moments.*

Look at Marie Forleo. She shared the Oprah stage and has since built an empire.

It's incredible.

So, if you could only use three words to describe Amber, what would those be?

OPTIMISTIC (Hence pancake flipping and right-on-time moments), ENERGETIC, AND APPROACHABLE.

Is there anything that you want more out of life so that when your kids look back at you, they can say, "Wow, Mom blessed us with this legacy?"

When we set goals for the business, we set realistic goals and big-vision goals. There was a point down this entrepreneurship journey when it wasn't really working yet, but there was also this moment of 'it's going to work out and going to happen.' I feel like from a business legacy perspective, keep stepping into action and those right-on-time moments. With the connection of family, I think about those personal elements and the thing that's further off because we are going to travel more and go back overseas. We're doing these things and sharing this with our children as a part of our legacy. To travel and experience different cultures, learning how people live and what we can do differently. At the end, I see us having a small house with grandkids running around (hopefully). It comes back to family, community, friendship, and connection. If I boiled it down to one thing, it's focusing on what matters. I hope my kids say, 'Mom loved people hard. She supported people, was there for people, and loved us; she did this for us.' It comes back to how are we loving on people? I hope that's pulled through in so many different ways.

This makes me think of the GOAL cards you all send out in the mail. I have mine still on my vision board. It may be a small piece of paper, but man, does that small piece of paper mean the world!

Callie, I have all my GOAL cards since 2008! How they come true when you document it, see it and step into it.

All those cards are your markers. If anyone asks about your milestones, there they are.

What is your definition of a female entrepreneur?

Someone who is creating their own future through their business. Ultimately, a better business means a better life. We can run our businesses well, and when we create something that gives us the peace and freedom that we want, we can serve and support so many people from that.

Complete this sentence…What if I?

> *"Ultimately, a better business means a better life. We can run our businesses well, and when we create something that gives us the peace and freedom that we want, we can serve and support so many people from that."*
>
> *Amber McCue*

I ask myself this question all the time: 'WHAT IF I QUIT?' I ask myself more through a positive lens than what it sounds. Am I doing the right thing? I get a gut reaction, and if I'm like, 'no' or 'yes," then I throw that one out. I think at times I was taught not to be a quitter, but what if I do? That helps me tap into what do I really want? Is this the right thing?

I know I'm not alone when I say this, but it's also asking, 'Will I be disappointed in myself? What if I didn't give myself the opportunity? What if I didn't step into the next realm? What am I missing out on?'

What am I missing out on, and who do I still need to serve? Do I still have something that I need to personally do here? For someone, for myself, for my family? Sometimes the answer is, 'no, you don't need to do anything else.' Then, the other times, the answer is, 'you can't quit.' The voice comes back and then you know. You might not know what the next step is, but you know you have to keep going.

This is *"Come Sweat or Silt."* Will I stop or will I forge ahead?

BUILD YOUR OWN DAMN LADDER

Meet Ryann Dowdy, CEO of Be in the Room, Business Coach + Author

Ryann Dowdy knows a thing or two about playing the sales game. After spending over a decade helping corporations generate millions of dollars in sales revenue, Dowdy realized it wasn't enough. Today, she stands confidently teaching women how to sell in a way that feels GOOD!

Most recently, she has created a space for women who want to rebel against the status quo, UNCHECK the boxes, and toss the superior ladders out the window—to build new ones.

Ready to ditch the 9-5? Allow Dowdy to show you the way…

△   △   △

RD: *Who am I? I am a wife, a mother, and an entrepreneur. I grew up in a suburb of Kansas City, then moved to New York for college as a division 1 athlete. At the time, whatever school offered the most scholarship money and was furthest away from home, that's where I wanted to go.*

I had somewhat of a normal life experience. After I graduated college, I moved from New York to Florida with a friend to start my career. I thought I was going to be in public relations, however, I landed in sales. Overall, PR, advertising, and sales

were really not that different, yet when someone said yes in sales, you got paid commission!

I don't usually mention this, but my very first sales job was doing phone sales for one of Lou Pearlman's companies (obviously before coming out as a conman and serving jail time). It was my first day on the job, I had a one-call close, and I came home with $200 cash. I was hooked! I was a recent grad and thought $200 was big money! Over the next several months, I started to see the writing on the wall and that what we were doing wasn't exactly ethical, so I left and began selling radio advertisements. After selling radio and TV slots, I then made my way to the digital realm. In 2011, digital marketing agencies were on the rise, and I found myself playing in the startup space!

In 2017, I wanted to start a business. I went back to work after my son was born and realized my dream role as a Director of Sales for digital marketing agencies was—meh.

I began networking, talking to people, and met so many amazing women. I was seeing a trend in new businesses that were struggling. I would hear things like, 'It's going okay,' or, 'I'm having a hard time with xyz.'

I realized sales was a pain point! Nobody was teaching sales. Most people hate it. I was really good at it, and it was something that came naturally to me. That's when I started helping women leave their 9-5 and build their businesses.

In 2019, I left my job, and my new business skyrocketed! Then, I partnered with an elite coach, and her and I began a new business together in sales. Now, I'm reinventing myself again!

CK: What do you think was the most profound moment in your career that really made you pivot, coming from the 9-5, to *it's my turn to run my own business*?

RD: *Our digital marketing agency was backed by investors. The board was filled with successful business owners that joked that the agency was their private plane money. In reality, they didn't need it. I had that moment where I had to ask myself, what was I doing busting my ass for these men who didn't give a shit? They weren't mission-driven, nor did the business mean something to them. (Please don't misunderstand me that people with money are bad people.) I love money, and I love people with money, but I have found that I work better when my heart is in it. I was emotionally attached to my work, the team that I led, the clients we worked with, but they were not. What was I doing pouring my heart and soul into this business? I was missing spending time with my six-month-old son at the time and the rest of my family. If anyone was going to buy a private plane, it was me!*

CK: Hell yeah! I have been in a similar position where I was part of a group that was put together for lucrative purposes. When it's somebody else's dream, yours gets lost in that. I think a lot of us can relate. No matter who you work for. But you have to have the clarity to say, *I'm not climbing their ladder anymore.*

Amen.

Have you ever found yourself in a situation that has not been good for the growth of your career?

There was a client of the agency who was a jerk. He would only work with attractive women. He wouldn't work with our VP because he was gay. He wouldn't work with his account manager because she was a little heavier. He treated us like shit and we kept taking his money because it was money.

That was not okay. At what point is the amount of money not worth the way people are treated? I personally was never involved in that exchange, but I watched it happen. You did not want to put me in a room with that man because I wouldn't have bit my tongue. Just because he was a client didn't make him superior in any way, shape, or form in my mind. That was the moment when I said, 'I'm not doing this.'

Good for you! Before you went into entrepreneurship, did you ever see yourself stepping away from corporate and leading your own gig?

No. I was the kid in the group project that always said I'd do it, so it got done right. Even a year or two before it happened, Callie, I thought there was no reason to become an entrepreneur. As a salesperson, I was already in control of my own income. I even remember saying, 'That role is a lot of risk. Why would I take that risk? Let the other guy do it and I will still get paid commission no matter what.' Until one day, I woke up and realized I did not want to do what I was doing anymore. At first, I thought I would change industries. Maybe marketing had just run its course, and I needed to play in a different space. Until I moved into entrepreneurship! I thought if that person could figure it out, so could I!

Did you know right from the get-go that sales were going to be your genius of choice for your entrepreneurship journey?

Not at all. It was actually Jen Sincero's book, You are a Badass, *that encouraged me. She wrote that everybody needs a coach. Initially, I could have used a coach when I was 23 years old. I was out of college, getting started in my career, and I didn't know where to go for advice. My mom lived 1500 miles away and was never overly career driven. I couldn't complain to my boss, and my friends were also broke, not knowing what to do in their own careers.*

It was out of that thought process that led me to my first business as a life coach for young women—women who were coming out of college and getting started in their careers. It also came from conducting many interviews when I was the Director of Sales at an agency. I noticed there was a huge difference in the way young men presented themselves versus the way young women presented themselves—to the point where it pissed me off! Why are we not equipping young women to better handle themselves professionally?

I spent nearly seven months in that space until I became aware of two things: your audience does not know yet that they have a problem (they are too early on in their own career to see the writing on the wall), and young people don't have a lot of cash.

Why was I good at negotiating salary? Why was I good at being able to sit in a room and disagree with everybody in it and not lose my shit? It really came down to having had my career in sales.

I think that's how it works sometimes. You leave something you're good at, only to come right back to it. For years, I was a PR and marketing rep in luxury sports and represented all kinds of athletes. I left that arena and went into personal training. Now, I'm practically back doing the same publicity and partnership work

that I was before, but this time, I'm on my terms. As a leader in our businesses, we get to choose. We get to choose this time. And the work means more to you.

Watching your business grow in the last couple of years, what do you think is the biggest difference in how you were operating before to currently?

I was never in an industry that was overly male dominated. But, at the time, sales was always taught by men. It was very masculine, the numbers, the logic behind what was being taught. What I have learned is that sales is actually extremely emotional. It's extremely relational and about connection, so the biggest change that I've had to make is that I'm still teaching the same material, just in a way that's more aligned with me and who I am as a person. It's not just a numbers game. I'm still pulling out my corporate PTSD where we don't have to make 100 phone calls a week. My team and I are able to have difficult conversations. It's not butterflies and rainbows all the time, but it's heartfelt. I love my people and care about them. I want them to be successful, to hit their goals and dreams. In the corporate world, I didn't even have the awareness to ask questions like, 'What do you want to get out of your job here?' It was, 'What can I get out of you?' Now, with my employees, it's, 'What can working here add to your life?' That's been such a big flip for me.

That's huge. In the last two years, we've seen that shift in the corporate world and more employees going into entrepreneurship. It's exactly what you said: *what value is there left?* It's become a culture of *how many hours can they get out of me* and *what can I do to cover their asses?* But, at the end of the day where are you?!

I've had to let people go, but I've learned how to do that from a place of respect and compassion. Again, those were never things that were taught or talked about. Even though I was never disrespected in any major way, I still never had an example of what respect, compassion, and connection look like in an employment environment. Creating employment is important to me. I think a lot of companies treat their people like shit, and then they can't figure out why nobody wants to work. We're in a space where people are saying, "Nobody wants to work, there are no good people." There's plenty of good people; they just want to have a space where they can be seen, heard, and understood. They just don't want to work for you. The proverbial you. The you that overworks and underpays in your industry, that takes advantage of overtime laws and never pays up. That's who they don't want to work for.

Hands down. That's exactly what it is. You and I have both been in those environments, unfortunately—and fortunately. It also led you and I to where we are right now, knowing that there was something bigger and better waiting for us.

Why don't you tell us about that?

community i tit i th

We are referring to it as a peer led mentorship organization specifically for women of action. Just badass women who get things done are really who we want to serve. This came out of the type of conversation that you and I are having. We have advanced so much in the career space—there's more women starting businesses and more seats at the table. The wage gap is getting smaller, but we are finding that the higher we climb, it can be kind of lonely. We don't know where to look for a model, and it's harder to look for connections. I kept hearing from women at a certain level of success that they don't connect well with others because of the fact that they are such high achievers. I've seen that, but I've also seen that the rooms these women walk into were based on their job titles, the amount of money they were making; were they an employee? Were they moms; were they not?

Why do we keep doing this? Why do we keep putting women into boxes just so we can all look the same? If we would just lock arms with all of the badass women of the world who want to rebel against the status quo, that's where true change can happen. Be in the Room is a community for women who want to rebel against the status quo, women who are looking for identity and connection, ideas and collaboration that are not based on income, title, or industry.

Is this for women all over the United States? How are you connecting? What does that look like for your vision in this new business?

We are officially global! We have two members in Canada, so we get to call ourselves global!

We are connecting virtually with an in-person component. This is such a heart project, a passion and true purpose project. I'm really walking in faith and counting on those opportunities presenting themselves. It's just one foot in front of the other.

You have to get there first. For somebody that has left a partnership and decided to wipe the slate clean, what would you tell that person about taking the leap and starting from scratch again?

Granted, all our journeys are going to look different, but what do you do when you try something from the ground up?

It's interesting that you say that because I told a couple of people I was starting over. And it's actually not true. I'm just changing direction.

You're pivoting.

You never go all the way to zero. We think we're starting over because it is a new career path. You still get to take everything with you that you've learned through all the experiences. Yes, I'm starting a new business from the ground up, but I now have a network, I have a community, and infinite knowledge. You're not leaving everything behind unless you want to—I never wanted to leave it all behind, I wanted to bring it with me into the next.

I think when you're thinking through a pivot or a change, take what serves you and leave behind what doesn't. Even if it was a bad experience and was terrible, what did you learn? My corporate experience wasn't incredible, but I learned some really amazing things. I met some amazing individuals and even now, I'm leaning on those relationships with what we're creating with Be in the Room.

Never downplay all of your experience. As a business example, a lot of people will want to be in a position and say they've never done that work before. Don't forget that just because you didn't have the job title you're walking into or starting doesn't mean you don't have experience that's relevant. All your past experience brought you into this for a reason. Find your people! Callie, you and I have connected in many ways. How we met and connected to our friendship now. Find people that you can go have a cup of coffee with, Zoom, or even pick up the phone. Because trying to do it alone—which we tend to do as high achieving women—is an exercise of insanity.

I love that! An exercise of insanity! We find ourselves in burnout or pure exhaustion—you hit that wall and you're like, *WTF?!* Has that been your biggest learning curve in this, or do you feel like you've learned some other things along the way that have helped you say, 'I got this?'

> "Because trying to do it alone—which we tend to do as high achieving women—is an exercise of insanity."
> *Ryann Dowdy*

The most important thing I could say is that it's not a mistake. And every time you learned a way that was a mistake, you just didn't learn the way that worked for you. Because again, high achiever, former athlete—there were mistakes; we made mistakes. There were literally errors that were tracked on a clipboard. They were reported and were our stats.

Or recorded! Even better!

The biggest thing I've had to learn was that it's never an error. It's just a way that didn't work. I can say that I've made mistakes in business, and I have, but none of them were nearly as detrimental as I thought they were at the time. It's all a learning curve. The only way we fail is if we don't grow.

You're a mother, and granted, we all know our kids tend to challenge us in more ways than one, but what do you tell your kids when they feel they've made a mistake or somebody else has told them their work was a mistake?

That's a really great question. My kids are just now old enough to where I am choosing my words very carefully. My two-year old will say, 'I can't do it, Mommy.' And I'll say, 'Yes you can. Maybe you have to ask for help, but you can do it.' My son is learning to write; if he thinks he did it wrong, I'll remind him he's still just learning. It's little things like that. It's not wrong if you've never written your name before. I'm not perfect, but I try to be selective with my words when we talk about mistakes or what didn't work, so we try again. I'm always asking different questions in the language. [TR31]

I get it. Looking back at my experiences as a young woman growing up, and now having been through what I've been through, I wish we were taught more personal development. What a difference that could have made if we learned it so much earlier in life! You do find yourself sending your kids a different message even from what you've been taught. It's not wrong, our parents just didn't know what they didn't know at the time.

My mom and I talk about that all the time. I went to school on a volleyball scholarship, and I quit my sophomore season. The coach that recruited me wasn't the coach I ended up playing for because we weren't a good personality match. My mother was devastated when I left. It was like a job that paid well, so what was I thinking? I told her I didn't sign up for a job. Now, when my mother and I have that conversation, she tells me 'I would never give you that advice now. If you are in a job that you hate…'

Get out!

You just know better, do better. Even when I'm projecting feelings onto my children, I try not to tell them, 'You make me happy.' It may sound good, but it's not their job to make me happy, right? It's my job to make me happy. My favorite thing to say is, 'I love being your mom' instead of, 'You make me happy,' because I never want them to feel like it's their responsibility to make me happy.

Along all our entrepreneurial journeys, we all decided to choose better at one point or another. I truly believe in my heart that we found that inner grit, that personal brand, whatever that may be for each of us. What do you think is yours? What does true grit mean to you?

It's never giving up. True grit is being told 'No' 27 times and still showing up! My freshman season of volleyball, we went 3-21. Do you think we stopped practicing? No! We weren't allowed to.

We just ran harder. Even when it feels like shit, even when it feels like you're not winning, and can't do anything right, you get up and you do it again. That's true grit.

I have this old, framed message that I got from my mom a long time ago, and I still remember what it says. It has a flower on it and the message says, 'I get up, I fall down, but meanwhile, I keep dancing.' That's exactly true grit, YOU GET BACK UP. You get back up because you're not going to allow yourself to stay down no matter who tells you no, no matter who tells you, 'You can't do it.' It's not allowed. You're going to push through that.

What's next for you?

World domination, clearly. (LAUGHS). I want to spend the next 12 months having fun in my business. Doing only the things I really enjoy doing. My word for the year is RECEIVE. Which means allowing more of the feminine energy and more flow. The masculine energy served me very well for a very long time, so what's next for me is to really have a lot of fun. The big picture is what we're building with Be in the Room. It's the women who were told we were too much, too loud, too opinionated. It all ties back to adolescence. This is something that is going to serve young women, and I don't know exactly what that is yet, but I do know they won't have to wait until they are in their mid-30s to realize what's been told is not true.

Describe Ryann in three words!

Direct, Opinionated, and Badass.

What is your definition of the female entrepreneur?

This is where my left and my right brain start battling it out.

Everyone starts working together (LAUGHS).

My definition of a female entrepreneur is a woman who has control of her life.

It makes me sad to think of the women who don't have as much opportunity.

Or that don't even know that the opportunity exists. That's why I'm so on fire with everything Be in the Room. You and I—everyone featured in this book—we knew that the room existed, or somebody introduced us to the room. There are people out there that still don't know that the room exists, and that there are other choices. They still live in a reality where entrepreneurship is told that it's not for them, they're not smart enough, they're not good enough, or it's too risky. There are so many women who get inundated with that programming.

Who introduced you to 'the room'?

Lauren Golden. She is the Founder of 'The Free Mama Movement' and a dear friend of mine. She was launching her movement back in 2017 when I was antsy and unsure. She teaches women how to freelance so they can stay at home with their kids.

Do you have a mantra or quote that you live daily in?

It's changed. I was told a long time ago that the harder you work, the luckier you get. I shy away from that because if hard work were enough, we would all be successful and rich.

My mantra, in general, is, 'You only fail if you quit.' Hard work is necessary and there is a certain element of work that we have to take action, but like I said, if hard work were enough…

Between all the work, how do you find yourself recharging? I know you love to read, as do I. I'm good for an actual book in my hand and love turning the pages. I guess I'm old school like that. Spending time with family is fun, and planning those activities, but at the end of the day, you do need your YOU time. What does that look like for you?

It's primarily exercise and my morning routine. I burn energy through exercise. What meditation is for some, I solve a lot of the world's problems walking, boxing, or cycling. I get up before the rest of my family, usually between 4:30-5 a.m. It is my favorite time of day because it's quiet. I'm sharper in the morning. I take time to read, to journal, and to pray. It's that time by myself before my brain takes off to the races. My morning routine is very important for recharging, even though it seems counterintuitive to get out of bed earlier. I find that when I skip that routine, sleep in, or have a sick kid, my day is off kilter, and my energy is low.

Ask me what I could do all day and never get bored at? Sitting in coffee shops and talking to people as they rotate through.

As you and I have done on multiple occasions!

GUT CHECK

Meet Cara Clark, Owner and primary Certified Nutritionist of Cara Clark Nutrition + Co-Author.

Cara Clark's passion for nutrition began at a cellular level as a college athlete, high performance was priority! But it wasn't until she started mentoring sororities that she realized she was being called to help pave the way towards new behaviors in health coaching.

Today, Clark takes a "non-dieting" approach with her clients across the globe, introducing challenges through her member based CCN Challenge groups, helping celebrities, Olympians, and pro-athletes along the way!

Most recently, Clark has been featured as a co-author with HGTV's Christina Hall in their book, *The Wellness Remodel: A Guide to Rebooting How You Eat, Move and Feed Your Soul*, as well as being featured in Carrie Underwood's *Find Your Path: Honor Your Body, Fuel Your Soul and Get Strong with the FIT52 Life*.

Sharing her approach to wellness and nourishment, let's meet Cara!

△ △ △

CC: *My story and how it's come full circle is a little bit ironic. When I started in nutrition and what it has come to be—it really wasn't a direction I wanted to be in. I didn't have this grand weight loss story that a lot of people in the field do, or a fitness journey in that regard. I hadn't really opened my eyes to what drew me into the nutrition world.*

At the time, I was 24 years old and had started my business. My husband, who was also a business owner, helped me align those steps. He helped guide me to my audience and the direction of going back to school to study to be a registered dietician or opening my own business as a certified clinical nutritionist. I thought my college career in basketball and other sports had led me here. I played basketball all four years, and was always thinking about potential, and how to consume proper food for energy—there was just zero information on that. Today there is more, but it's still very limited in the performance world, and a lot of performance nutrition related work is to sell supplements; that's always been disheartening to me. For a long time, I really hated supplements because I felt they misguided athletes. It wasn't about what supplements you took.

After I was married and got pregnant, I started to understand my real passion in nutrition. It was about performance, but not athletically. It was performing and feeling good so you could achieve the best version of yourself. I knew that my passion grew so much deeper than I originally had thought. I didn't know how—GOD hadn't totally revealed that to me—but I knew that it was more than the science of nutrition. I knew that it was mind, body, and spirit. It was then revealed to me that I had actually been suffering from Disordered Eating after basketball. How could I fulfill the identity crisis I was going through? As career long athletes, how could all of us transition poorly into regular life? All we ever knew of ourselves was athleticism and performance. So, my identity crisis went to controlling food, my workouts, and obsessing over them! Trying to achieve a body type and mindset that was really unattainable is how minds of athletes can work. I hate to lump sum all of us, but I've talked to enough people to know that we spiral out of control a little bit when we lose that identity. I started to understand the mind was more about losing my identity and replacing that with control.

Then the question was, 'Who can relate to this and who can I relate most to?' I started working with sororities, emailing every sorority local in Orange County/Long Beach area. There were so many responses! At the time, three out of five sorority girls were suffering from eating disorders. I was able to work with and help these girls break the cycle before they ended up where I was: completely obsessed. I was able to help them understand that exercise is supposed to feel good and support your entire well-being, not to punish you for your lifestyle choices. I taught them that when women actually slow down our exercise works better for us. Not only does it give us the kind of mental energy we need, but we also feel more balanced; it helps us hormonally and to burn fat better. I was also teaching a sorority boot camp and then would take the girls to the grocery store (this is pre-kids when I had all the time in the world) and teach them about food labels. We would walk the store as I showed them why we wanted to choose foods without labels and how eating colorful means more vitamins, nutrients, and antioxidants, and how those delay oxidizing our bodies (meaning aging).

These were high-achieving sorority girls. Potential business owners, future doctors—very ambitious. They had been doing the same thing I did: starving themselves and trying to achieve somebody else's body while being faced with the challenge of Southern California culture. When they started to support their own bodies', energy needs with real food and workouts, they started feeling better. These amazing women, who were anywhere from four to six years younger than I was, were able to get through school having better energy and support for their bodies. I'm really thankful that I went that direction, and it swiftly changed when I started having kids. I had two kids in two years, which led me to stop teaching the boot camps. It was a little heartbreaking, but I knew my time there had come to an end. I couldn't manage it. I couldn't even wake up that early in the morning anymore. I actually had a higher risk pregnancy during my second pregnancy, where I was not allowed to teach fitness. Sometimes, I feel that GOD diverts the direction physically so that we can get to where we need to be. That's when I kickstarted my current business, primarily focusing on nutrition.

Soon after, I quickly had two more kids. Four kids in five years. I was able to manage growing my business, hire employees, and every year, I was doubling or tripling. I had four employees, and nothing was really set up to strategize and run a functioning business. It was all based on quick needs—stop and put a Band-Aid on it. After being pregnant and nursing, growing a business for seven years, I started to *have my own physical problems. I always say it's GOD's way of getting your attention. I've always heard the quote, 'your body keeps score and it always wins.' But that could never be me! Because I did everything right. And I really do live what I teach. I exercise at the pace I need to go. Unfortunately, that pace changes as you get older, and I wasn't even acknowledging that. I was still pushing it really hard, getting up at four in the morning every day, and then four years ago, my system started shutting down. At first, I was like, 'This can't happen to me.' My ego was way too big to be sick. How can I teach and be the sick one? This was the wakeup call of adding the spiritual and emotional side into what I teach. Some people may think that's more subliminal and that's all they hear. They only see what they need.*

My sickness started at the time I had my four-year-old daughter. It was my third child and she was also sick. She was bloated, had red on her eyes, skin rashes, and got every little bug that was going around. She was turning into a sickly little kid. When I was working through it with her, I was learning about how the whole body is related and how it connects to our environment and emotional well-being. I felt like what we were going through should be a part of my educating others and how the philosophy of food related to all the above. Sadly, we have to go through the fire sometimes in order to be better teachers. I've trusted that what I'm learning through motherhood is what I'm supposed to be teaching. Claire, my daughter, is always my greatest teacher because she's my most sensitive kid. She's very sensual and emotionally aware. For some people that's really hard, but I look at it as a gift. Once we got her healed, I was able to focus on why my body was shutting down.

I found out I had been dealing with functioning mono for about nine months. It was a lightbulb moment of clarity as to why I was feeling so bad. I started working with different functional medicine doctors to help my body heal itself because I knew it was capable of that, and there was going to be a great teacher that would show me how.

Then, insomnia kicked in and my skin started breaking out; things were really falling apart. I had eight employees that were all stay-at-home moms who were able to operate their talents with CCN, and I was so proud of that. I couldn't shut it all down because I had people relying on me as well as clients. It was that wakeup call I needed to begin working with one of the girls that came to my sorority boot camps.

She had claimed that it changed her life and that if it wasn't for me, she would have never gone the direction of teaching Chinese medicine, practicing healing the whole body. And so, it was full circle that she opened my eyes at one of my sessions, revealing that I was very spiritually weak. I responded that I was one of the most spiritually sound people she would ever meet! I never missed church, prayed every day, and taught my children faith. As far as faith goes, I am it!

It was a wakeup call in how desperate my body, mind, and spirit were needing to feel connected. I was teaching it and thought I was doing it, but there were so many things I was missing. I didn't expect to have this story. I expected to be full-go my whole life, always achieving and always in a mode that was energetic. I didn't expect to be the sick one.

Going through all of that helped me to be more patient, understanding, and realize how important it was for people to open the door to connect those dots themselves. Because this isn't something I can tell people that is going to work for them, they have to work through it themselves. Everybody's fire is different and unique, and so I get to be the enabler of supporting them going through the hard times uniquely as they go through it.

I started a protocol where I shifted my diet a little bit, really pulling back my workouts. I had a bedtime, turned off my phone at a certain time, and I had to sleep in until the sun came up, which was incredibly hard for me. This really shifted my entire way of thinking. I was able to heal, and it took me about nine to 12 months. Which again, with my ego, I was going to heal overnight because I was superwoman! I was able to provide a different outlook to clients that really needed to work through their own healing. I started talking a lot more in my programs about healing, and they understood that. Understanding meditation and prayer life, and connecting the dots to mental, emotional, and physical. I had to go through the fire myself in order to be able to support all of that. I love the full circle part about my client, Sheila, being the one to open my eyes.

When you have talked about the grit, I had to forget the grit and stop hustling. I had to stop working so hard, trying so hard, and allow things to naturally play out the way they are supposed to. I had to surrender and accept it. To give up that four to *six o'clock a.m. window. I'm sure that looks very different than a lot of other people's hustle stories. Because mine was the opposite. I had to slow down to educate nearly 800 subscribers and tens of thousands of people who have done my program. I could help them understand just how much pain they are inflicting on themselves by going too hard. I had no issue going hard! I had an issue slowing down.*

CK: I think the word "hustle" is overused now. Like you said, we find ourselves in these life moments that cause us to slow down, or we have to really pull back in order to take care of ourselves. As female entrepreneurs, we are all guilty of trying to wear all the hats.

Exactly.

Do you feel like when you were taking that time out for you and tapping into new spiritual practices, that that was one of the biggest transformations for you along this journey?

It definitely was. At the time, I didn't even realize how it was supporting my business transformation. I just thought it would open my personal transformation. I didn't think I would ever end up sharing it because I thought it was that personal. I realized at one point, that GOD allowed me to go through it so I could help others go through it themselves. Rather than using water to put out their own fires, they would walk through it themselves. It was very eye opening and transformative. One thing led to another, and I found myself surrounded by other entrepreneurs that were going through it also. I was able to give my testimony and share the pain of slowing down. It was completely transformative for me and for my clients who I shared that with.

If you were to look back at everything that you have been through leading you up to this point, is there something that you wish you would have known in the very beginning that you didn't know then?

"I realized at one point, that GOD allowed me to go through it so I could help others go through it themselves."
— Cara Clark

I'm not a deep thinker in the sense. I have never gone back to figure out what could have helped or made that experience easier. That's a really interesting question for me, because I do think sometimes people go back and say, 'Yeah, I wish I would have known xyz.' However, one thing I wish I would have known is how bad those morning hours were for me to work 6 a.m. to 8 p.m. I still have to have that first part of the day, but I could have organized it differently. I wish I would have realized the hustle isn't supposed to take away from your sleep. LOL.

But it does…LOL.

Actually, I never even saw myself as a working mom, much less with a company of this size that reaches women throughout the entire world. The reach is international. This wasn't my deepest desire. My deepest desire growing up was to play basketball in college and to have a big family. I did and had that. I didn't have a deep desire to run this mega business or to create. I knew I'd always be a writer because I've always written, but I didn't realize being a writer would be running a company as well. For so long I didn't even want my children to know that I worked, so I would hide it. I wish I would have understood that childcare doesn't take away your ability from being a mother; in fact, it just helps it. I wish I would have had less ego and been able to support my own needs through motherhood better by asking people for help and hiring help. I wouldn't even get a house cleaner for the longest time because I was too proud to struggle at anything. You know what I mean? I was six years into motherhood before I would even hire babysitters to work. I just had too much pride to not be able to do it all. But again, I wouldn't have gone through it the way I did had I understood it better, so there's really no regrets. (Besides the sleep part).

What you just said kicks me in the stomach—that you felt guilty telling your kids you were working. For female entrepreneurs who are mothers, in whatever capacity that is, we strive to find the 'balance' because we do want to be successful mothers, business owners, a part of the family, and in partnership with our loved ones. But, who loses out in the end? I think that's what sometimes stops us.

It certainly doesn't open up the ability for plan and structure. I think that's one thing that really suffered with my business—that I didn't have a plan and structure. I was literally letting GOD run the show, which is a great thing, because he was sending me the right people. I also had to keep low overhead because I was starting my business with no investors; I'm sure you know that part too. You have to buy into platforms and have systems; that all costs money. It's very scary as a female entrepreneur. Half of us are doing it just so we can financially support our families. The time I gave myself to work did not allow for systems and structures and really turned out to hurt me and my business. One suggestion I have for female entrepreneurs is to invest in the time and money that systems and structure allows.

Your business now, how do you have it set up? How many employees do you have, and what systems are in place so that you can still be Cara *and* run a business?

I had to spend a great amount of money. I hired a CFO, an outside consultant that helped me run the business and get everyone in the right seats. He was on for two years straight and now comes back every year or so to do an evaluation. I have one full-time nutritionist that also helps develop meal plans and recipes, and another recipe developer who also does executive assistant work. Our jack of all trades does graphic design, helps with Pinterest and other media. I also have a full-time executive assistant, we call her Director of Operations now. She runs the back end of the business. My husband also helps with that while he runs his own business. I have a Challenge Operations girl who manages the project of every challenge, a designer, an editing team, a trainer, and three photographers.

That's why the food looks so good!

When I do collaborations or page promotions, someone always says, 'These photos don't look the same as they do on your Instagram.' It's because I paid for those, and you can pay for those too! LOL.

Our trainer coordinates the programs for the fitness challenge; her name is Tammy. She's not on staff. But we also have a marketing girl who helps to strategize and run new projects—to funnel those out so we can reach more people and the right people are getting their foot in the door.

The next big pain point for me in all the growth was keeping the integrity of the community. We grew the community overnight and it was amazing. We supported each other and the goals of what CCN is. I didn't want to lose that integrity by writing Carrie's book and then producing my other book. I had to get myself set up to where we could keep the integrity of the group and it wasn't about people just coming in for weight loss, meeting their goals, and leaving. It's never been about a diet plan, so that was important to me.

What would you tell others that are seeking to step outside their path right now and pave their own way?

That's a really good question. I would tell them to do some self-discovery on what their goals are. Don't try to be somebody else and run your company like the one you see on Instagram or the one you think you see. Really get aligned with what your goals are.

Now that you are running your company and have your team, what do you see for CCN in the future? What is the next step?

We would really love to grow our subscription. Our subscription is not only the best value of what we offer, but it's where we get to go the deepest on education. We realized the social media platforms are great, but you can't really teach. Because you don't know who's reading what, and so in order to understand the science of nutrition and the component of the full body wellness that we add—with the mind, body, and spirit component—you have to be really learning as you go. Our subscription goes in-depth, and that is where our desire lies. We like to be able to learn it ourselves so we can go on to teaching it. I really see it growing by 5-10k people that are really engaged in whole body wellness, so we can really help change lives.

I don't love the subscription model and how hard it was to get here, but now that we're here, it's fun. This is not something I can just show up on an Instagram live and teach on because viewers don't have the understanding that our subscribers have.

Do you still work with clients 1-on-1 at all, or do you just work primarily subscription-based and with those that come into your program?

We have two on staff wellness coaches that work with individualized clients, and that works for now. I do not personally take individual clients unless they are professional athletes. Because of the time consumption and because of all the programs that we do have.

Let's move on to some fun questions… What are you feeling grateful for in this very moment?

Just more time with my family. My Julys are MY Julys. I've always calendared time in to just be at the lake. My husband and I use a term called 'carefree timelessness.' For example, you have no idea what time it is, but you're just going with however the day leads you. I wake up happy, and I go to bed happy, and I'm just grateful that I can be with the family and not worry.

You're definitely on lake time because lake time is a whole other time!

Aside from the lake and getting away for family time, where else do you go, or what ways do you spend time to recharge Cara?

Meditating. It's something that I work towards every day. I always say keep your feet on the ground and your head in heaven. That's how I live my days, to be in that stillness. I'm not somebody that can relax watching TV, so that's how I recharge and reconnect.

Three words that would describe you?

Driven, Passionate, and Faith-Filled.

What is your favorite scripture?

Jeremiah 16: God says, 'You will go where I send you and say what I tell you for I am your Lord. You will follow me.' That's always been really relevant in my life and, at times, I feel questioned and challenged, and God says, 'Nope, we're going this way! You'll find out later, or maybe not, but you need to trust me.' For me, it's about trusting deeper.

For me, it's Jeremiah 29. I know it's a common one, but it's been around me since I was a child.

Is there anything that you want more out of this life, for you? You've already done so many great things, but is there anything you want more?

I am completely content and satisfied. I have a hard time with work opportunities because I really don't want things to change—I really love my life. I'm in a happy marriage of   years and have four healthy children; how could I ask for more? I know that maybe even sounds cliche, but there's nothing I want more of; in fact, maybe even less of some things. LOL.

Reel it back!

I really do think some people have that desire to be on TV, to live in LA, and do the New York thing, and that's not me. I want a cabin in the mountains. I want to be more recluse, if anything.

We also do the lake thing, but I would love to have a place in Colorado!

Exactly. I might do Eastern Tennessee just to keep it really simple. I just love time away and being in 'carefree timelessness.' Being in nature and doing nothing.

I was on this big hike one year in Colorado with this group of women, and we had hiked a fourteener. We were at the very top of a mountain, and I found myself just sitting in pure silence with the mountain range all around me. It's like you said: to take pause and just be—be still in those moments.

100%. I feel like it's easier to be still in the moment when you're in the mountains. You're kind of lost, you don't know where you are, ya know?

One of the things I introduced to my clients in the last Wellness Remodel Challenge was forest bathing. It's being out there without any devices or distractions, no music, and just watching the world go by. That's why I like living in the South. People just literally sit on their porches and watch the world go by, and there is still so much to be said about that.

It's a very sweet and humbling thing that we can still do when most of us don't.

Exactly.

Last couple of questions! What is your definition of a female entrepreneur? What does that truly mean for you?

What it means to me is that if you dream it, you can do it. I guess another mantra I live by is, 'do what makes you out of breath talking about.' There's something where people literally get out of breath because they love talking about it so much and are so passionate about it. But that's not what they are doing. I think so many women are dreaming, but then there's things like fear and finance that hold them back. **Women are the life changers, the game changers, not the rule followers when it comes to business.** *So, if you dream it, you should do it.*

Complete this sentence... What if I?

This is hard. LOL. What if I could teach people that there is joy in the imbalance and the imperfections. It is so genuinely what I want: to help people understand the joy is part of the journey, and it is not the end game. **We have to experience the joy in the pain and in the imbalance because there is no such thing as balance—the joy is in the imperfections, because we were not all made to look like Cindy Crawford. We are who we are, and accepting our genetic code is part of that.**

CLOSING THE GAP

Meet Kelly Pascuzzi, Founder of Creative Living, philanthropist, and Co-Producer of the film, *The Ravine.*

Most people have no idea that their true potential is truly magnificent. Just ask our next leading female entrepreneur, Kelly Pascuzzi.

As a life and results mentor, Pascuzzi has led the field with two globally renowned programs as an award-winning consultant. Over the years, she has helped catapult others to success under the Proctor Gallagher Institute, working side-by-side with her mentor and human performance phenom, the late Bob Proctor.

Most recently, she was a co-producer of the award-winning Hollywood film, *The Ravine.* Based on real-life experiences, *The Ravine* weaves a story of evil, hope, and the afterlife.

Read below as Pascuzzi shares her journey of intuition, new beliefs, and how to expect the impossible.

△ △ △

Looking back at your life to where you began and where you are now, what did you originally see for yourself?

KP: *I think I always had a knowing that I was placed here to teach in some regard. I'm not sure that I had an exact picture of what that would look like, but I did always have a knowing I would use my voice to teach—to possibly bring awareness to people in regard to having certain ideas.*

When you talk about teaching, I think back to when we were little and were asked what we wanted to be when we grew up. Was a teacher in your line of sight, or was there something else?

I don't think your typical idea of what a teacher was at the time was even the vision. I think it was just a knowing that I would use my voice to educate and teach in some way.

I think as we're younger and have those instincts, it's interesting to see how we project ourselves around others. Were you the leader of the pack? What was your position in a group of friends?

I was more quiet and observing. I was always wanting to make sense of things and make sure there was peace and that everyone was getting along.

Now, having said that, as a mother of three boys, do you feel like you have continued to play the peacekeeper role?

I think early on, but then I had an awareness that I do not have control over those kind of things. I can only control how I can respond to the activity and the energy in our home.

If only we would all grasp onto that...(LAUGHS).

I'm not saying it's easy, but I did have an understanding that I would never be able to control these young men in the sense of what they would think, say, or how they would respond and act. Now, I know I was never supposed to because they are their own expression. They are looking at being creative in regard to the direction of their big ideas and dreams.

Let's talk business. Tell us where you started in the working world. The majority of the collaborators in this book began in corporate and then left the building! What was your experience?

I began in a corporation as a customer service manager. I ran three different departments. Then, I noticed the hours I was working were not going to be in alignment with having a family. I was recently married, and so I decided to make a shift and go into recruiting. I started recruiting individuals from college campuses to go to the financial services industry. I really had fun with that because I enjoyed the interaction and connection with others. Then, I shifted again and stayed at home, making that decision to be at home with my boys. That was probably one of the best gifts I had ever given myself. In the last five years, I really started asking myself, 'What is my purpose? What was I placed here to do? How can I make an impact?'

I got involved with coaching. I do results coaching with individuals and corporations. I started my own business and loved the opportunity that I had to make a difference in people's lives. I was able to introduce them or awaken them, one idea at a time, in walking towards living the life they truly desired.

I think a lot of mothers can relate, especially those that take that time out—to carve out space to stay at home with their kids. At some point, you've decided to be in that chapter with your children, but then on the inside you begin to think, 'What about me?' What do you feel was the biggest nudge in that for you?

I was asked one time, 'Are you the star in your own film? Are you the star in your own movie—in your own life?' When we were filming The Ravine, *there was an awareness of, 'Am I really the star in my own film?'*

I had the habit of encouraging my husband and my boys to go after their big dreams: that they could be, do, have anything. But I think the nudge was, 'Are you living what you are preaching?' I had to be honest with myself. I was not really expressing who I was placed here to be. There is such a fear with stepping out into the unknown. I always liked that place, or so I thought I did. I'm aware now that when I'm there, I'm not growing. I have gotten very comfortable with being uncomfortable, knowing that I'm growing as I step out and start to express those gifts that are within me.

What would you tell someone that is in that place of being uncomfortable with growing?

I would tell them there is a lack of understanding—that you're always growing. We're either growing in one direction or the other. If we are not moving in the direction that we want, we're usually going backwards in life.

I could not agree more. We talk to so many people throughout our lives and we hear others tell us, 'I don't like change,' and they've put themselves in that box. They're comfortable in the box. But from a coach's point of view, and especially in your business now, you're trying to nudge and awaken them to experience something new.

Your coaching business, how did that all come into play, and who are you serving?

My husband and I have always been students of personal development. However, I knew there was a missing piece. I had noticed when you went to a seminar, read a book, or listened to a podcast, the results were temporary—they weren't permanent. We had an opportunity to attend a live event with my mentor at the time. When I was listening to his teachings, I realized that this was the missing piece. I wasn't aware of anyone else that taught paradigms like Bob does, and what I love is that he goes to the root of the cause. It's really the understanding of how to permanently change the paradigm so the behavior changes permanently.

When I say paradigm, it's nothing more than just a multitude of beliefs that become fixed in our subconscious mind that are controlling our behavior. The majority of our behavior is habitual. When I was introduced to this material and started working with the ideas that worked for me and the changes that were happening in my life, I wanted everyone to have the same understanding in regard to offer new optionality in their lives.

After attending the conference and being introduced to his teachings, how did you all connect? What made you step over the line and create that shift for yourselves and your family?

A couple things. First of all, we all have one of our higher faculties known as intuition. There's a nudge, like you said, a voice and understanding that you are supposed to move forward even though it doesn't make sense at the time. So, we acted on that. There also was a knowing that we cannot continue to think and behave the exact same way that we've always been thinking if we want our results to change. We had the desire for better results. We knew that everything could be better, even if it was one percent more a day. If everything can be a better version of ourselves, only by one percent, think of how differently your life could look. So, we've always been open to pursuing that, to studying ourselves, and becoming more aware of who we really truly are. It takes a committed decision and desire to want to grow. Like you said, so many people feel that they are comfortable, and they like things just the way they are. They're just not aware that things are always changing.

Let's talk about how you educate people with the tools taught in the *Thinking into Results* program. What does that onboarding process look like?

I believe it's important for my clients to have a first-class coaching experience that is unique from anything else. The material, topics and coaching we provide at Creative Living go much deeper into what is causing a client's current results, getting clarity on what they really want and all the tools and resources to get them from their current level to their desired level. The combination of the topics our clients learn and the way we teach it allows them to experience sustained results instead of falling back into old habits.

I have many touch points with my clients throughout the 13-week program to provide a welcoming environment, accountability, community with like-minded individuals, discussion and feedback opportunities. I really believe accountability is the insurance policy of success.

You can change your paradigms (limiting beliefs) in two ways:

Constant spaced repetition through elite coaching or emotional impact. Usually, the emotional impact is something very negative. That could be a loss of income, a loss of relationship, or some other devastating event.

With Creative Living's elite level coaching, my clients experience massive transformation that has a ripple effect in every area of their lives. This is because how you do one thing you do all things.

When someone goes through the entire program from start to finish, and they have committed 100% to doing the work themselves, what can they expect as an end result?

They can expect to become, to do, to have anything that they want. I know that seems far-fetched to some, but it's actually true. I believe the most important thing that they will get out of the program is an understanding of what they truly want. If you would ask 97% of the population what they want, I believe that they would not be able to tell you what they truly want. They're possibly telling you what they think they could do—what they know they could accomplish because it's things they've done before, but very few people allow themselves to express what it is that they truly want. Because we're so programmed through logic, we don't even allow these ideas to surface and miss them because we don't understand the how. They would walk away with that and understanding the universal laws.

How does it make you feel when you see your students graduate from the program?

I feel I've made a huge difference and impact when I see students going through the material, working the ideas, and the results begin to change. It's so rewarding. But I would never say that they graduate because I believe we are never finished with this work. We're always continually growing in our awareness. As we grow in our awareness, that's when we begin to understand what we're truly capable of. The only way to gain awareness is through study and application. You're never done studying. My mentor, the late Bob Proctor, t i for 50-plus years…

I think there is a piece to even be introduced to it. But I also think there is a piece to owning the material.

What do you see for the future of your coaching/training business? How many times a year do you offer this experience?

I work a lot with corporations, so the timing is based off what is best for their team. I also coach individuals. I run multiple sessions/courses, so I am very specific as to when I run those based on my schedule.

Do you see this expanding in any way? In-person retreats? Or is there somewhere you want to take this part of the business and run with?

I have really big ideas for this business. I am in business for myself, but not by myself. I am in business with facilitating Bob's material. I really consider this a movement. I really believe after the pandemic occurred that people have hit the reset button and are starting to ask themselves not, 'What am I doing,' but 'Why am I doing it?' I don't think there is a better time to be sharing this material because people want different results, they just don't know how to get them. I've heard multiple individuals say, 'I've tried that before.' But they've never tried these teachings because I guarantee you these are different—they solve a problem. They actually change the behavior permanently.

I would love to have women's initiatives and retreats. I do think there is such a need in the corporate world for this material. What I'm finding in employees is that they are going to work just to work. They are not having any fun. However, when they can go to work and are emotionally involved in the big idea or goal as a team, there's huge satisfaction in their lives.

YES! I think back to some of the other interviews that I've conducted thus far, and that topic has been brought up more than one time. That employees are feeling the value in what they can offer the company and vice versa. The pandemic was a real shift for the corporate world.

I believe now more than ever that if the corporate world isn't working, or who you're working for isn't a good fit, make a change. There are so many people stepping outside of that into entrepreneurship, trying to find something that helps them feel like they are doing life with purpose.

I so agree. There's something inside of them that is looking for expression. We all have this (I call it the power flowing to and through us), this energy. This potential power that is looking for direction, and we have to say yes to these ideas to express them. So many people are conditioned to suppress those ideas. They have been conditioned to have the thought that, 'I should be satisfied with what I have.' I am grateful for what I have, but I am not satisfied because I know I have more to do. I always know there's a better version of me, and there's more work that I have to do to become who I was placed here to be.

What would you tell someone that knows they were meant for so much more, but they just don't know how to take that step forward?

I would encourage everyone just to accept the idea and say yes to it. What I have found, which is freeing, is that my responsibility is that I only get to decide what I want. I'm not responsible for the HOW. The HOW will be uncovered as I am moving towards the direction of this big idea. It's always delivered at the exact time that is needed. I used to think the goal was to get—to achieve. The purpose of the goal is who you become in the process. I would encourage everyone to say yes to whatever it is that is looking for expression, knowing you don't have to know the how; you just have to decide what it is that you want.

That's where the journey takes place.

I think we look at the journey and ask if we are worthy of it. What we need to ask is, 'Is it worthy of us?' I had to really be aware of working on my self-image and originating for the first time who I wanted that to look like, who I wanted to be, and what I wanted that to feel like. I believe we grow in our awareness of who we are and then are easily able to say yes to big ideas because we can see ourselves accomplishing those things.

Let's shift. This book is about what we have been discussing—those moments of digging our heels in the mud and saying, 'I got this!' Climbing ourselves out of the trenches or having sat in a pile of our own tears, and still believing in ourselves enough to continue. Was there a moment in your life when you felt you had that moment of grit?

For sure, I've had many of those moments in my life. My moment of grit was when we were producing the film, The Ravine. *It was a really big idea to be involved with. We knew we felt a calling to share this universal message with the world of hope and forgiveness. We didn't know how we were to do it because we had never done something like that before. There were many moments when we were faced with some really big decisions that required a new way of thinking. What was happening in the external did not show evidence that we were on track with this film or that people understood the reason and calling behind it.*

We could have put our hands up and say, 'We quit.' We were so emotionally invested with this big idea that we knew, no matter what, this was going to happen. I think all of us have experienced points in our lives when we felt like quitting or giving up. But maybe that was an idea that we really weren't as emotionally invested in? When you are going after a big idea and you are willing to do whatever it takes to make it happen, you will. A higher faculty that I call 'the will' allowed us to go to that place many times in regard to the film, knowing that we just had to keep moving forward and everything would take care of itself.

Do you feel like that was the hardest part of getting the film out there and sharing that message?

At the time, we thought that was the hardest part. When you're in the thick of it, you think it's the hardest part. Then, you're introduced to the next hardest part. What I have found is adversity really introduces you to your other self that you weren't even aware was inside of you. It brings something out of you again that you were not aware of. When you are emotionally locked into something, you're determined to see it through. It was what I would call 'a calling' for us; we were willing to do whatever it took and refused to quit.

That is the purest definition of grit that I have heard.

That definition came over tears, frustration, fear, and all of the above. Now, we have the fun part to look back and see how all the puzzle pieces came together. When you first start on these journeys, you just have the one piece to work with and you have to believe that if you are moving in the direction of what you want, each piece that you need is going to be supplied at the exact time that you need it.

> "What I have found is adversity really introduces you to your other self that you weren't even aware was inside of you."
> Kelly Pascuzzi

Tell us the synopsis of the film.

The Ravine is really depicting a scenario of the unthinkable, unimaginable, of many lives being disrupted. And, coming to grips with what that might look like moving forward and making sense of the unthinkable. It's really a journey that I believe is going to cause the audience to really pause and think—possibly to consider different choices in their lives in regards to what real forgiveness looks like.

The word 'hope' is a universal word that we hear. What does it really mean? What does it look like and bring in the wake of tragedy? In the wake of raw, real grief? How do we get to the other side of that?

I've always had a desire to start a foundation or do something for those that are left behind.

Last time you and I spoke about the movie, you mentioned that you didn't have a cast the week or so before shooting? How does that happen; tell us about that?

Going back to the grit. We personally financed this film and had quite a few decisions to make in the process of producing. There was a time where we were 30 days out from starting production. The crew, trucks and all, were going to New Orleans to prepare to start filming. We did not have one cast member at the time signed for the film. Our team in LA contacted us saying that we were going to have to pause. We were determined to continue, so we said, 'No, we are absolutely not pausing. We know that the cast is going to show up at the exact time they are supposed to show.' That was on a Friday, and by Monday, Eric Dane, who plays a lead role, agreed, and signed onto the film. Then, it was one after another.

Looking back and talking about making big decisions, if we would have paused, the film would have never been completed. Who knows how long production would have been and how long it would have taken to actually complete the film?

They thought we were crazy!

It's like when you say you have that emotional connection to something so deep and you know you are supposed to do it, there's not a gray area for you to walk away. It's an absolute, and your gut is telling you, 'This is it! To hell or high water, whatever that looks like for us.' You've created a beautiful piece out of

this that ultimately is going to be a part of your legacy. My next question to you is: what do you want to be known for, what would make you proud? What does your legacy mean to you?

I would be most proud to be known as the person who accepted the idea and said yes. Without knowing the how, but I also would be most proud to think that I did everything that was absolutely asked of me. When I think about the film, one of the greatest compliments we could have ever received was that we did absolutely everything that was asked. When you know that you did EVERYTHING and didn't leave anything on the table, that's a proud moment. It was overcoming so many overwhelming beliefs (we had never produced a film), saying yes and moving forward without the HOW.

Really look at some of the decisions you've made and have said yes to you in your life— think if you would have said no to those opportunities. Things disguise themselves sometimes and come in the back area of your life. You may not really be paying attention to some of these opportunities. They require hard work and are not easy, but when you say yes to an idea or know that you are supposed to express yourself, that's when you can be the most proud of who you've become.

POWERHOUSE PARTNERSHIPS

Meet Dr. Melinda Dunn, Medical Director and Co-Founder of GLOSSRX, A Micro-Aesthetics Bar

You are allowed to be both a masterpiece AND a work in progress. So, why not be both?

Dr. Melinda Dunn never intended to play small; it didn't serve her. Years of cultured programming followed by modern society led her to a decision that would land her in one of the largest multi-billion dollar industries worldwide. Today, Dunn can be found serving as Medical Director and Co-Founder in one of Kansas City's most affluent neighborhoods, leading facial symmetry and anatomy with medical aesthetics. Her keen sense of artistry met with her certified credentials has authorized Dunn as an exclusive injector and owner, building her business, GLOSSRX, from the ground up.

Beneath the gloss of success, this mother of three knows a thing or two about unexpected outcomes. But, when it comes to anti-aging, rejuvenation, and going against the status quo, I'll let her be the one to tell you.

Here she is.

△ △ △

CK: What comes to mind when I ask you what your definition of what the female entrepreneur is?

MD: *I have to wonder how many females actually go out thinking, 'I'm going to be an entrepreneur!'*

Some of us have placed ourselves in a position where we know we can do better, and at some point, we finally pull the plug and go and do it.

I also think there are people who have always wanted to be an entrepreneur and are in a similar situation like I was where you don't like how this is going, and you know you have a great idea that pushes you into entrepreneurship. As females, we have a nurturing side. There is something in us where we generally care about the output. Where financial success is measured in dollars and cents. We truly want to do something to be able to give to others and do our best. We know we are capable of making people feel happy, and at the heart of our service, we do that, and we do it really well.

CK: I feel very fortunate that you and I are both in a city that is in the Top 10 of female entrepreneur-based cities across the country. That's huge! Prior to you getting started in your business, was there any mentorship or leaders that you already looked up to or that helped pave your way?

MD: *I honestly can't say that there was because I never thought I was going to own my own business. I didn't see myself being an entrepreneur.*

I would watch females start their own 'hustle,' but it looked as if everyone was figuring it out as they went. Maybe it was my lack of networking in that arena because it was not an area I thought I would ever be in. If anything, it was a level that I wasn't prepared for.

For example, if there was a multi-million-dollar business that was leading a workshop, that's not a level where someone who is starting from the beginning should necessarily be. This person may even be asking, 'What is an LLC?'

However, I did have someone that gave me insight into what it was like to be in the medical spa industry. She was one of the most open individuals I've met in that industry because I also have met a lot of people who were very closed in and who did not want to share for risk of competition or what not.

Describe your process in starting your business: what that looked like for you, where you came from, and the challenges you felt during?

I always knew in some essence that where I was was not going to be where I ended up. I went to medical school right out of high school and had parents that were very education oriented. When I was accepted into the UMKC Medical six-year program, there wasn't a discussion as to what I was doing or where I was going. I was already there. There wasn't a big decision that had to be made. Even entering med school, I was hesitant if this was something I wanted to do. I loved law—maybe I would have gone into law school.

What I knew about myself was that I was a hard worker, so no matter what I did, I was going to work really hard. Even today, I'll have people comment on my credentials and intelligence, but I always respond with how much I learned along the way and the effort it took.

Everything I do, I always put 100 percent in. I'll never walk away; I've always just allowed my circumstances to show me when I'm done.

Once I finished residency, I took a little hiatus and did ER work. I knew I would probably end up in traditional medicine, but I wasn't ready for it, and it didn't seem very appealing to me at the time. In medicine, you go to med school, residency, and then get hired by a hospital or a group and start seeing patients because that's what you have signed up for. At some point, I knew I had to experience that, but I wasn't overly excited, so I did my own moonlighting and worked in rural ERs. I was recently married, and that lifestyle wasn't conducive to having children. I had always said I wanted to be home and help my children with their homework.

> "Everything I do, I always put 100 percent in. I'll never walk away; I've always just allowed my circumstances to show me when I'm done."
>
> Melinda Dunn

So, I took a job working at a regular, traditional hospital—St. Luke's—and it was good for me. I experienced what it was like to be a standard family practitioner in a good hospital with good colleagues. I went from working full-time to part-time. The culture of medicine can be a bit challenging. When working with my patients, I tried to be very thorough, taking each circumstance and situation to heart when making a decision. I worked four days a week; however, I was easily spending time working 6.5 days a week. By then, I had given birth to three children and was going to quit to see how else I could practice medicine.

Another doctor asked me if I had ever thought about a job share. I never had. But it changed my life.

It kept me in medicine. I don't know if I'd be practicing medicine today had she not given me that opportunity. I was sharing one position with another female doctor, and we worked in a clinic that was very accommodating to working mothers.

After pivoting, I had a female colleague that said to me, 'You can either be a good mom or a good doctor.' I was taken aback. It was like, 'How is this even possible? I know I'm a good doctor and I'm trying my best to be a good mom. So, are you saying I'm a bad mom?'

It was so disheartening. Why would a female do that to another female? I don't know.

Working part-time was the best thing for me. I was surrounded by other great colleagues, and it kept me in that arena. I loved what I was doing, but there was a part of me that looked at the future five years down the road, leading me to question myself asking if this was it?

Part of my decision in choosing to leave traditional medicine was the culture and what was demanded of me. That is another discussion. I felt like a robot at work. I was at a point where I just needed to know who my next patient was and ask the questions. And that's not who I was or am. The pressure to deliver, to perform and see x number of patients, documenting the way they wanted me to and check the boxes they wanted me to check, that got to be the reality.

Some people navigated that system very well, but I didn't.

That's when I wanted to learn about giving Botox in aesthetics. I freelanced giving injections and fillers. This part of the industry was exciting to me! Even though I was being trained in this area, I still didn't know what I would end up doing with it.

It got to the point where I had quite a bit of people calling me asking if I could give them Botox. They were stay-at-home mothers, or they just liked the convenience of calling me and getting it when it was convenient. The weekends served me well in this practice. I thought I should slightly advertise and see where this could go!

Next, a friend of mine introduced me to my now business partner. She had no medical background; she loved the aesthetic industry so much and had invested in another clinic that didn't go well. That clinic was liquidated, and she was still adjusting from that experience. By the time I met Stephanie, I knew this was something I was going to do. I was ready to leave my work and do injections.

Right out of the gate, I asked her if she wanted to do this or not. When I said, 'Do you want to do this?' I meant, 'Are you ready for this ride because this could be the biggest mistake of both of our lives,' but I was not afraid of risks. You fail enough times in life, you don't fear it anymore.

That's how we started. We started planning, and I thought I would shift to part-time, as I was still in traditional medicine, but then I didn't even want to be at that job. When the pandemic hit, I reevaluated where I was putting my time. I told my work I was leaving and that I was going to open a med spa. What was interesting was that many of my colleagues supported me in this decision. There was a part of them that knew this wasn't the end for me.

They saw the writing on the wall for you before you were even able to act on it. Did you feel like you were crossing the line over the square box you had put yourself in?

Something about me knew I was never going to be in that box. I wasn't meshing with that culture. If I really like something, then I put my everything into it. I was asked to join medical committees, and I had no interest in doing that. I literally wanted to go to work and go home. That was my life. 'Work' was a generating-revenue sort of situation. There were moments where my authentic self would come out, and it was clear that the box I had put myself in was not for me. For some people, it is, and they thrive in it!

Your colleagues were telling you to fly!

Yes! The people who saw me for who I was knew that it made sense. My mother is a very traditional Nigerian mother. According to culture standards, I shouldn't even be working. I should be at home raising children even though I was a doctor and went to school.

I know others can relate to this. Different cultures can have various lines of vision for their loved ones, as you mentioned with your own mother. Knowing what has been taught, and now it's your turn to carry the torch. Did you ever feel that pressure to say, 'Mom, this isn't going to be for me?'

It's interesting. My father, who passed away in 2009, raised us girls to not depend on anyone else. So that part is ingrained within me, thanks to my father. However, my mom is very old school and conservative. She very seriously assumed I would probably go to medical school and get married to a doctor. Of course, she's always been proud of me, and she's proud of what I'm doing now, but it wasn't in her plans for me. Even today, she will say things to me like, 'Why don't you have dinner made already?' The maternal things that were never me. I married a great guy who knows me very well, and he doesn't expect these kind of things. Well, for one, he's never seen them out of me before. LOL. So, there is no expectation for that to just change, but when my mom comes around, it blows her mind. It's as if I'm disrespecting my husband.

She went to school to learn how to garden. She was raised very well in Nigeria in a very affluent family. And the women were really taught how to be great wives. My mom does have a nursing degree and did go to nursing school, so she was 'pushed.' But first and foremost, in that culture, you are a good wife and mother. That's very important to me as well, but what else is there for me? What about my capabilities? I still feel like I sometimes get pushback from my mom on how busy I am and the things I decide to do. There's always the 'why are you doing it?' kind of situation. Sometimes I have a hard time explaining it because I am working more than when I was working in the hospital.

I want to show my kids that this can be done. I want them to have that impression on females. Then, there's another side of me that would like other females to see that there is nothing about me that is incredibly special, except for the fact that I just tried. *That I can build something with my own hands and control the direction in which it is going. I love being a wife and mother, but I can also do this too. There is something in you that you know is not satisfied. Even when you know it, you may not even be paying attention to it.* But it's also important to know that not everyone has it, and it's not important for everyone. We have to respect that.

What would you tell another female that has faced similar challenges? What would you say if they came up to you and said, 'Hey, you've been here...any advice?'

I think the saying 'you can have it all' is not an accurate statement. I feel like there is an invisible pot. And, in order to increase the contents of this 'pot,' I have to take away from another pot. My sister is an example of this when it comes to children. She went to school and did it all on her own, finding success that way. I have a husband who can take care of the home front if I'm not there. But even then, I still have guilt.

So, what does it really mean to have it all? I don't know that I have it all, but I do know that when I'm happy and excited and doing things, building things outside of my family and having those conversations, I feel like that is a good thing for my kids to see. I always hesitate to say I'm a better mom because of that. I guess we'll find out when my kids get older. My kids are very young, and I don't want to speak too soon (LOL). I would like to think I'm an acceptable mom (I don't have teenagers yet), but I guess we'll find out!

When I've been on maternity leaves, I have found myself counterproductive. However, when I'm busy and moving, I'm moving with them too. My children see endless possibilities.

When someone says, 'There's nothing you can't do,' there really isn't. That's something my dad instilled in me. There's a good chance you may not succeed at it, but it doesn't mean you can't do it. There is always a way. There is no impossibility out there. Anytime someone asks you something, instead of saying no right away, say, 'Let me think about that.' Because there's usually a way.

It's so true. I love what you said when you asked your business partner, 'Are you ready for this?' In this book, we talk about female entrepreneurship being a roller coaster ride, and you better be ready for it! That being said, you're not always going to be ready for the uphill battle in front of you. Talk to us about how the business got started. You really, truly built this baby from the ground up.

In fall 2019, we were in the planning stages. We were figuring out how this partnership was going to work and starting a clinic at the same time.

We wanted to do everything by the book. Getting the LLC and lawyers on board, legal fees; I'm the physician and she's not. Opening up a medical clinic in Kansas, everything was a process. The lawyers we used originally had a medical division but didn't know how to work around the idea that we wanted to open up a medical clinic in Kansas that's not entirely owned by a physician.

The biggest thing was creating the entity. Then, it was what kind of services do we want to offer? I wanted to just do injections and have an injection clinic, and she wanted to have a medical spa. Then, we were on the train of, 'You run the medical spa, and I'll do the injections.' But, when you open up a business together, you both have to be open to new strategies.

We knew of places on the coast that were our inspiration or things we wanted to embody. As we began looking for business locations, we had to ask ourselves how much money did we really have? We wanted to do this out of our pockets and didn't want to go get a business loan. As the search continued, we felt like our dreams started getting smaller and smaller. We were so tired of looking that we nearly signed a lease at a location that would have been a disaster! We just wanted to get started!

This is when you trust your partner. There was something in Stephanie that was holding back. I am the kind of person that commits to a decision and rides it through! And, if this is where we were going to be, I could be happy and make it work. But she wasn't. There was something about it. I think I had asked her a question and realized she will always be second-guessing if this was the right decision.

I knew we couldn't be both in this 100 percent if one of us had a question in the back of our minds. I was ready to accept that. I needed her to be in a 100-percent place because we were doing this together. Yes, at the time I was frustrated, but I couldn't ignore that she felt that way.

Right. It had to be a hell yes for the both of you!

So, we didn't do it. It was now February 2020 and then what happened in March of 2020?

Had we signed that lease to start in March, we would have had to pay rent on a place where no revenue was going to happen for six months. Again, two things I learned: trust your instinct, and respect your partner's opinion. Stephanie is more of a cautious mover! We both have our impulses, but I had to listen to the fact that if we are going to make this what we want, it's a two-way street.

Fast forward, Hawthorne Plaza was a place where we always wanted to be. We had already looked at Hawthorne and didn't make the best impression the first time! I think we literally got off the tennis court and showed up to the meeting. So, we decided to go back and see if we could make it happen this time.

That's when my husband stepped in and said, 'Go big or go home. You're not in your 20s trying out a new hobby. If you want to do this, do it now.' Again, I'm not afraid of failure because it's just what you do if you try. So, we went ahead and went for it! From the moment we did it, everything felt right. We knew it was the place we wanted to be.

On the back end, we were still working with our lawyers on all the details. Even though I was trained in this area 10 years prior, I hadn't been actively up to date so it was like I was learning a new industry again. I didn't think about it at the time, but I was teaching myself an entire new specialty in medicine on my own.

I also think that is what holds people back. Like you said, you are in a new industry that has kept going without you in it and is constantly creating a variety of new ways and techniques. A lot of times people think they have to know it all to jump all in.

Truth be told, for entrepreneurs, you're going to jump all in because you're betting on yourself, but you are also going to allow yourself to get the work done no matter what.

You have to know that about yourself. There were times when I asked myself, 'What am I doing?' You don't even think about how much you don't know; you just start learning. You take one step at a time, look at the problem, and say, 'Here's how we're going to fix it.'

I was back to taking notes like I was in med school again, understanding the intricacies of facial anatomy—it was a crash course. You have to be open to always learning.

The other side of that was that I'm learning about owning a business. That's another degree on its own.

Stephanie was learning as well. Her background is in marketing. She had a short experience with the medical spa she had invested in, and now we were doing this one together. There are so many questions, for example: taxes?

Do I have to pay those? LOL.

We went down a lot of tunnels that led nowhere. You have to back up a few steps and start again. It's one thing, one moment, one step at a time. We divide and conquer very well. Her strengths are my weaknesses, and things I'm strong at give her that opportunity. We learned this about ourselves as we were in meetings. We'll be in meetings with vendors about products, and she may not be saying much, but then I understand their language and vice versa.

So important when you're in a partnership. You have found the ebbs and flows of how you two work together, but what do you want your members and guests

to experience as they walk into your facility, this business that you two have put so much sweat, equity, and heart behind?

There's no shame in the fact that we did this ourselves. Therefore, I want our personality and who we are—for people to feel that when they come in. I call it a boutique medical spa in the sense that we offer services and products we believe in. We want our clients to walk out and feel great, but we also want you to be our friend. We want you to decide if we are the kind of people that you trust and genuinely would be friends with. We are just like you; this just happens to be something we do and can offer to all of us women.

Each client is like a potential new friend. That's something I've always liked about being in medicine. It's talking and meeting so many different kinds of people and hearing their story.

I always use the reference about salons and barber shops back in the day. They were places that men and women congregated in, not necessarily having any connection other than attending the same salon. I wanted a similar environment for us. We are your neighborhood Botox clinic—women come in and start having conversations, realizing we're all in similar stages of life and rising together.

I love that. We're all rising together because there is room at the table. We just have to sit at the same table.

That's a perfect way of stating that! All of us have our strengths. For instance, there are mothers at my children's school that are always volunteering. They may be stay-at-home mothers, but they have a full-time job volunteering at school, and I thank GOD every day for those moms because that is their strength. That's what they are able to bring to the table. They help out the children and the school, where that is not my cup of tea. I pick and choose the areas I want to help out in school, but some of these women constantly blow my mind in the sense that they give all their time to run these organizations and make this happen all for our children. I don't see them sitting at a different table. We are all in this together and that is what they are bringing.

In the meantime, I'm keeping everyone feeling beautiful. This may sound superficial to some. I'm keeping people feeling confident and reminding them that just because you are a mother, or a wife doesn't mean your time for yourself is over. You can still care for yourself and do things to keep that light shining. It just doesn't happen in our 20s and gets taken away. Let's do this!

For sure. What do you see next on the horizon for GLOSSRX?

Where we're focused right now is building our clientele and expressing who we are with all in our clinic. Even down to owning our beauty products. We want to make sure everything is medical grade as opposed to something you can get at the store.

We've crossed our T's and dotted our I's; we have the credentials and know what we're doing from that standpoint, but so do a lot of other clinics. This is OURS. We're really personally invested in this. We're always going to put out new ideas at GLOSS. One of my favorite ideas we've had is to offer ear piercing for little girls because they can go where their mom goes for facials and other beauty treatments.

In a boutique environnent versus a tattoo parlor.

Exactly. Not a Target or similar retail experience. We also do events, and not all of them are centered around aesthetics. I would like to have an opportunity where I talk to middle school girls about their face and caring for those things. Talk to them about their hormones, why they break out, etc.

Slowly and surely, we will reach those milestones in our business. It's always fun to have a new idea, but then you also have to think about the logistics.

We've all been down that road a time or two.

We don't want our clients to just walk in and walk out without socializing. We're very chatty here.

If you were to read about yourself, 30/40/50 years from now, what would you be proud to reflect on? What would that look like?

That's a good question. You're putting me on the spot, girl. I gotta come up with a good one!

I want to be a good mom. I want my children and family just to know that, but I also want people to see me as someone who did what she wanted. Who wasn't afraid of failure, who wasn't afraid of the status quo—of expectations. She competed with herself, and that was her biggest competition. Not other people. I want other people to come and bring whatever they have. Aside from being a good person, a good mother, and trusting GOD, people can judge me through my actions. I'm not good at saying, 'This is where I excel,' and 'This is what is good about me.' I'm the kind of person that if you know me and you see how I act, I'll let you make your own opinion, and through those actions, you know the kind of person I am.

ONE GUTSY MAMA !

Meet Julie Moe, Founder + CEO of Zooby Media, Creator of The Gutsy Mama Project

Here's to a woman who decided to "buck the system." From guilt-ridden mom to cashed-up mom boss, Julie Moe began her career on Music Row in Nashville with the industry's largest mogul tycoons.

Today, she is the proud founder of Zooby Media and has created a space where motherhood meets mamas launching Squarespace sites in the drive towards financial freedom.

Moe's marketing expertise has helped thousands of women run profitable Squarespace Design Businesses, all while scaling the ladder outside the glass ceiling!

Is it time to get GUTSY? I'll let her talk you into it!

△   △   △

JM: *I had never planned on being an entrepreneur, never planned on being a CEO. Growing up, I dreamed of being an Olympic gymnast or a Supreme Court judge—NEVER an entrepreneur. It was never something that crossed my mind until I was forced into it.*

I was working for a company here in Nashville, for a gentleman who was an entrepreneur. He had built the company from scratch to half a billion dollars. In

working for that company, I was their head of marketing, and I remember being in my Q2 quarterly performance review, standing across from my boss at the time (stellar performance review always cause that's who I am!). He said, 'Julie, you know what I like about you? That I can always count on you to tell it like it is. I know you'll always tell me what you're really thinking about—I do. Even if it doesn't necessarily jive with what the boss is thinking.'

That was my job; that's what they were paying me for. I said, 'It's funny that you say that because I'd like to talk to you about my place in the company and where I am going.'

I had moved up in the company and had been with them a long time. From the time they were a $30 million dollar company to a $500 million dollar-plus company. I could tell he was a little taken aback by the question. I don't think a lot of people sit down with their bosses and ask, 'Where am I going?' especially women. I didn't want to kill myself working my way up towards the middle in this company. I had been sort of stuck in the middle for a minute. And I remember he leaned forward and said, 'The best thing I can tell you is there's no place for you to go in this company.' It was a real gut punch because I liked my job, I liked the people that I worked with, and I liked being in the music business. I had worked for them for so long. So, I had to make a decision at that moment: stay someplace where there was no place for me to go or find another job. I started looking around Nashville and started taking interviews. Got offered some jobs and realized everything that was out there for me was lateral or more of the same. Upward mobility is what I wanted. It wasn't there for me in the job I was doing, and when I went looking for the job that I wanted, the company that I wanted to work for, it really didn't exist. I decided then and there to start my own company. I needed a company that had location and time freedom. Those were big deals for me! I never understood why you have to sit at your desk until 5 o'clock even if you are done with your work. If I'm doing my job for you, why do I have to sit at my desk?

Location freedom: FYI there's this new, amazing thing called the Internet where you can take your computer places and work from wherever, so why would it matter if I'm at work or in Paris?

I wanted to see what it was like to call my own shots—to be able to say, 'I don't think this is a good idea, so we're not going to do it,' where I hadn't had that before. So, I asked myself, 'What's that going to feel like? What if I could hire the people I wanted to hire? What if I could pick and choose the clients I wanted to work with?' And that is how Zooby Media was started in 2015. The hardest part about starting it was finding a name, so I named it Zooby, after my dog.

CK: What reaction did you get from others after starting Zooby?

JM: I'm pretty fortunate. I've made a lot of career changes in my life to wind up where I am and to be where I want. I think there was a certain amount of what I was afraid of: for others to be like, 'Here's Julie with another idea.' They've seen me do this and heard me say I'm going to quit a really good-paying corporate job in San Diego to move to Los Angeles to go to audio recording school at almost 30 years old. Because at 29, that was a good idea, and I wanted to be in the music business. So, I did.

> "I'm Gusty. For women in business, you don't need balls to start a business, you need guts."
> *Julie Moe*

For a while, I feared what other people thought. I compared myself to others and what they were doing. I kept in silence. I worked quietly after bringing in new clients. Before I went, 'Hey guys, this is my new thing!' I think that's something a lot of women do because we're afraid of what others are going to think about it. I realized later on down the road, I had this amazing support system, people who were like, 'WOW, that's awesome! How can I do that too?' That's when The Gutsy Mama Project was started.

I try to be successful at everything I do before I move on and into something else. You get to a point, and you say, 'I can do this. I did this. Now, it's time to find something that really feeds my passion.'

CK: Did you always feel like you were a born leader, or has your work experience led you into that role?

When I was 18 years old, I was a door-to-door salesman. I was one of those people that carried around a big bag full of products, whatever they had for me to sell that day. And from that job on, it was my job to take other people out with me and try to get them to sign up. My favorite part of the job, and every job I've ever had, has been the mentorship aspect of it. It's been training people—helping people. I have worked in recording studios, and to this day, my favorite aspect of that was hiring interns. Those interns who are now Grammy Award winners. It's the knowing there was a little piece of what I did, a little piece of hiring them in their first job and showing them how to make coffee (some of them didn't even know how to dial a phone with buttons) helped them on their journey to success. Having that mentorship aspect and trusting them to assist on their first session with a big-name artist has led them to engineering for major artists with Platinum plaques. That has always been the best part of my job. Mentoring the women who are younger than me to stand up for themselves in these companies and say, 'Hey, I've been with this company for a long time and I'm good at my job. I deserve a raise.'

Creating The Gutsy Mama Project has been the culmination of building websites and solving problems. The Gutsy Mama Project was my way of bringing everything in my life into one thing I really enjoy doing: getting to choose the mothers who come in and who are really going to be successful.

What's your process for choosing these women?

You have to watch a video and be very clear and honest. There is also a questionnaire. What are your goals? Why do you want to do this? Then, there's a conversation with me. Let's saddle up together, go for a little ride, and see if we're going to be a good fit.

I have members in The Gutsy Mama Project who have been with me for over a year now and they still show up every week to group coaching calls—and you jive with people. I wouldn't say I'm the coach for every mom, because I'm definitely the type of person who will hold your hand for a good, long time, but at some point, I'm going to push you out of the airplane with your parachute because it's time to go hard on your goals! There are people who need that. The moms that do really well inside The Gutsy Mama Project need a little bit of an ass-kicking, for lack of a better term. When I hired my coaches (all coaches have coaches right?), I said to her 'This is the place that I'm in, I'm stuck, and I need someone to kick my ass to get me out.' It's called The Gutsy Mama Project for a reason. It's not like a soft, hand-holding, healing, meditation sort of place. Let's get this done. Do I often recommend that moms meditate, absolutely! Do I personally meditate, I do. But, my job is to make sure they have the resources they need from The Gutsy Mama Project to be successful. They won't be winning Platinum plaques, but it would be really great to see them going on BOMB vacations. It's really great to see them happy because they can home school their kids, and their kids are thriving. Seeing the pros of having a $10,000 month, like OMG! That is such a magic number for an entrepreneur. That first five-figure month is such a magic number because you start to think, 'This is getting to the point where I could break six figures,' which is such a hard number for so many people. That six-figure number can be such a mental block for some.

What do you tell your mamas that have that mental block?

There's a question that asks, 'What do you wish you had more of in your life?' and for me, that's money. We're not supposed to say we want more money. I grew up very much with the mentality that money was bad, that people who had money were somehow bad. The Scrooge McDucks of the world, like Ebenezer. I just said McDucks—you can all tell how old I am (LOL).

That those are negative people, they're the bad people in the world, right? But here's the thing. I had to come to this realization, and I had to have my moms say this out loud, that money is good. Money will allow me to give money to charities, to save the animals. (I'm a big animal rescuer, I foster a lot of dogs). Money will allow me to save all the dogs. And, if I don't have that money to pay my bills or take care of my family, I will not have money left over to save all the dogs. I have to get a lot of my moms out of that mental block that asking for more money is bad. Asking a prospective client, 'What is your budget for this?' is such a hard question for people to ask. The hardest part for some people is realizing they are a business owner, who someone has come to for a service; therefore, they know they have to pay for it. Just say, 'What is your budget for this?' Money is an infinite resource. So many come in with this idea of lack. We're seeing it in the news. Unemployment is up, and people *are losing their homes. Yes, there are people who do not have a lot of money. However, a magic alien didn't come down when the pandemic hit and take all the money off of the planet. Every single dollar that was there before is still here, and it is entirely possible for you to take pieces of that. I've heard so many moms say they are terrible at sales. You're not selling them anything they don't need; you're not selling them snake oil. Their clients know they need a website. Every business on the planet needs a website. You not giving them a service is doing them a disservice. They're either going to have a crappy website that is not going to make them any money, or they're not going to have a website at all, so no one is going to be able to find them. You not going out and giving them everything that you can, selling your services to them, is doing them a disservice. You not putting it out to the world is doing the world a disservice. So, getting moms around that mental block is I think the hardest part.*

You don't have to be the world's greatest web designer to make money as a web designer. I will personally say I am not the world's greatest web designer, but I do create websites for people to have everything they need to succeed. I'm coming from a place as a marketer, and I build your website based on what I know your market needs. That's what I teach the moms.

What kinds of services and offerings are you seeing with the moms that come into the project?

The bulk of them are trying to help other moms. They're trying to help other female entrepreneurs, and I think they start there because it's a niche they understand.

They are their niche.

They are. It's easy for them to come at it with a real understanding. I have other moms who are coming at it from a copy standpoint. They came out of a job writing RFPs—proposals—so they write copy. As their coach, I want to talk to them about what matches their skillsets in this time. I do not have a problem going after the low hanging fruit because there is money in the low hanging fruit, right? For example, you come out of real estate, so let's talk about a website for a realtor. What does a realtor need in their site? Are there realtors that you know who need websites? Let's take the approach from: I'm not just a web designer, I'm also a person that has extreme knowledge in real estate, and I know exactly what you need on your website. I'll help them find their niche to get those first few sales under their belt.

There's this moment after you have designed your first couple of websites where you feel like you really do this. The clients are real and you have a portfolio of websites built. You see that shift when there is a post in the Facebook group, and someone booked another website/client! Or they sold another Squarespace template. I can feel that change, and we all dance because we are celebrating this money that is coming in for each other.

One of the first things I tell someone when they're starting their business is to go after your warm market. Go after the people who already know you're smart and talented, who love you and want to take care of you. It doesn't mean Great Aunt Ida needs a website, but it doesn't mean maybe the guy who lives next door who owns his own business doesn't. There's no better referral than Great Aunt Ida who says, 'My niece builds websites— you should talk to her.' Quite frankly, no one wants to go looking for someone to do that. They usually go with the first person they call. Very rarely does someone go shopping around for web designers! They just want to work with someone that they like, who they think will do a good job, and if you can do that, the referrals come in. If you are good, nice to work with, and fast, you will have a business.

Do you create your own personal sites since you have that experience and background?

No. I didn't start designing websites because I designed websites. I had a referral from a friend telling me that another friend (who didn't know exactly what I was doing) needed a couple of websites for artists he was working with, liking the looks of my work, and asking me if I could do something like that? So, I said yes.

And that's how that happened.

That's how that happened. I sort of lucked into Squarespace design. I really love it, and it makes a lot of sense in the way my brain works. It's creative and beautiful, and I can bend it really far without breaking it too terribly.

You know how they say you should have three things in your life? Something that is good for your body, something that is good for your creativity, and something that should make you money. I'm lucky because web design does two of those things for me. I will sit at my computer and try to figure things out. I love the idea that at the end of a project, you get to point to something and say, 'I made that.' That did not exist two weeks ago, and now this beautiful thing is out on the Internet and helping someone. It's helping a small business, helping dog walkers, helping recording artists look legitimate—whatever it is. I didn't just sell them something I'm not really sure they need; it's actually helping someone with their business. To be able to say I helped put something out into the world, my client is happy, and there are happier people in the world because of it, that's a really nice feeling.

You've worked with and helped major recording artists, but what would be your dream site? What would make Julie's bucket-list site?

I really like building websites for women. I'm very fortunate in that with the bulk of my clients, I attract that. I'm more than happy to have that as a niche of mine—the female artist, the female entrepreneur. I got a pretty big call this morning, so I'll let you know if I get it!!!

It could be a really good day…

I love getting texts from former clients. The call I received today was from an old mentor of mine who has a special project he's working on and needs someone who is reliable and creative, and the first person he thought of was me! Those are the most heartwarming and amazing texts to get!

I also built a website for a charity called 'Diversify the Stage,' which is about bringing diversity to the music industry, especially the touring industry. That was a really wonderful site to be a part of. The client trusted me and gave me free range and control. Diversifying is so important. You are literally talking to the only Filipino girl on Music Row! I get it! Those kinds of things that feed my soul and help others, I just love those. Where you're given free rein and you have an idea; make it happen.

It's more than just a passion project. You're serving that cause.

It's something I can believe in.

I always find it really interesting when you're in your groove, but conversely, what challenges you? Where do you find you get stuck at?

I am a very empathetic person. I have a tendency to take on everyone else's things until it feels very, very heavy. Until my lymphatic system is fighting, and I get stuck in fight or flight mode. I remember my coach telling me, 'Julie, you have to do this. You have to get into coaching.' I sent him this text saying, 'My family is depending on me, my moms are depending on me, I can't take it anymore. I can't do it. I can't do it.' And he called me. He never called me. He said, 'Yo! You are in fight or flight mode. You have to calm your body down. You have to stop.'

I'm one of those people where I get revved up and take on other people's problems. Sometimes I just have to step away. The day I got that call, my husband was working from home. I said, 'I'm taking two days off, and I'm not opening my computer. I'm going to lay in bed and watch trash television. I'm not going to worry about other people's problems for a hot minute; my assistant can help answer any questions in the group. I'll jump in if they need a coding question or a CSS question. I just need to take a minute.'

You do! I can relate; I'm the same way. I'm somebody who does come crashing down, and I crash hard. Like you said, it's fight or flight mode.

Obviously, we all love our Netflix and trash television, but what do you like to do to recharge?

I'm a big traveler. I was a traveler before I had my daughter, Roxy, and I'm a traveler now with Roxy. I try to get two to three stamps in my passport every year. My sister and I are planning our trips next year already. We are looking at Asia, Bali, or the Maldives, and I've got London on the docket this year. Travel is very important to me. Roxy has more stamps in her passport than most Americans. She's three. The beauty is I can work from everywhere. I've worked from Iceland; I've worked from Paris and Costa Rica. Having the ability to do that, to shut my computer and go walk around, enjoy the beautiful city, to stop and have a coffee in a cafe—I'm going to be that person. Travel is my vice!

What does your travel bucket list look like? Where have you not gone yet?

I haven't done Asia yet. I've been to several places in Europe and Central America. I would like to go to India. My husband has been literally everywhere already; he's a tour manager for artists. He really wants to take me to India. I would also love to go to Nepal and Southeast Asia as well.

It sounds like you're on your way.

That's the plan. I didn't really start traveling until I was in my 30s. I was living in San Diego, and that is like being on vacation all the time. I'm addicted! I love getting stamps in that passport. I don't like planning things; I don't do tourist stuff. When I went to Paris, I never went to the Louvre. I'm that person. I like going to a foreign city and wandering around. If you're hungry, you go into a restaurant and stop in and get lunch. I love exploring that way.

Do you like traveling with a companion, like your sister, or are you one of those backpack-through-Europe-by-yourself types?

I've always traveled with either my husband or my sister. For my 40th birthday, my sister and I went to Rome. That was amazing. My sister and I are excellent travel companions because we're very similar and very opposite. My strengths are her weaknesses, and my weaknesses are her strengths. Same with my husband since he's a tour manager.

You all have the system down.

He's got us covered. He's got a travel box with everything you could possibly need.

How long has he been a tour manager for?

Jeff has been in the business for thirty years.

He's a lifer then...lol.

If there was an all-star team for tour managers, he'd definitely be on that team.

Is there a place he hasn't been?

Jeff has been everywhere, but he hasn't seen. On our American bucket list, I'd like to take him to the Grand Canyon in an RV and take him up through Arizona and Utah, then all the way up to Yellowstone.

Have you personally been to Yellowstone? It's so neat.

I have. I've never really seen the National Parks since I was a kid. I'd really like to do that for him someday. We can also take Roxy when she's a little older and can appreciate it.

Speaking of Roxy—she's got you as Momma Bear, the go-getter—what would be something you would tell her in how to approach this life as she begins to envision her own dreams?

I've personally never taken the normal route in my life. I didn't finish college in four years; it took me like eight years because I was doing other stuff. I was living my life, and I wouldn't change a bit of it. My fiancé at the time dumped me and decided he wanted to be a recording engineer, so he moved to Arizona to go to school. So, I thought, 'Well screw you too. I'm going to go to audio school also, but I'm going to Los Angeles where there's a music business.' I was successful at that and ran a high-end recording studio, working with some of the biggest artists on the planet!

So, I never followed that path of where you get out of college and at 22, you get a job, work for someone for 40 years, and get your pension. It's never been my jam. I'm going to make sure she knows that that doesn't have to be her jam either. If she decides she wants to be a doctor and go to medical school to be a doctor for the rest of her life…amazing, I would love that. Every Filipino mother in the world would love for their children to say that! But I would never force her to do that. I also would not pay for her to not pay for her own things. When I was 18, I went away to university and my dad said, 'Go make some mistakes. We're here if you need us.' I think I would say the same thing to Roxy. 'Go make some mistakes. I'm here if you need me.'

With Roxy, every day we do affirmations. I think it's so important for people—women, children, everyone—to hear themselves saying nice things to themselves. We say, 'I am brave, I am strong, I am smart, I am kind, I am loved, I can do anything.' Now, I just say, 'Roxy, what are you?'

'I am brave.'

'What are you?'

'I am smart.'

'What are you?'

'I am strong. I can do anything.'

She's almost four, and it's my job to fill up her bucket of self-esteem so full that no matter how many holes someone punches in it, it never goes dry, it never goes empty. When she can walk into a room and say, 'I am brave and strong and smart. I deserve to be paid. I deserve to be respected,' I'm hoping I've raised a young woman who finds all of her validation internally instead of externally. I don't want her to care how many likes her Tik Tok received.

I love the analogy you used with the bucket and the hole theme. I think that is so important. When we hear each other saying negative things to ourselves in a joking way, we quickly have to pivot that.

I used to be a very self-deprecating person. Then I realized if I'm saying these very negative things about myself, why shouldn't someone else? So, I stopped. I'm not a self-deprecating person anymore. I will not make jokes about myself; I will not make jokes at my expense. And I will not talk about my body, my face, my hair—whatever it is—negatively in front of my daughter because she sees everything that I'm doing.

And they soak it in! I'm a huge advocate in teaching younger kids, especially females, to not get thrown into the 'program' if they can help it.

Absolutely.

Speaking of affirmations, what three words would you use to describe yourself?

I would say I'm loyal, probably to a fault, but I don't mind it. I'm very straight talking. I'm that friend when you break up with someone, I'll ask you, 'What do you need from me right now? Do you need me to hate their guts—'cause I will— or do you need me to be kind of soft about him because you're not sure how you really feel?' I've been that friend that's straightforward. When my friend broke up with a guy and I said, 'Yeah, that guy's always been horrible for you,' she was like, 'Really?' That's not what they needed in that moment, and you're like, 'Oh! You still like him, my bad.'

I'm Gutsy. For women in business, you don't need balls to start a business, you need guts. I was nine and being bullied. A kid was walking behind me, making fun of me. I remember his name; it was Nathan Wilson, and I was at Shadow Hill Elementary School. He was teasing me, and I turned around and slapped him across the face. I thought, 'I won't put up with this from anybody. I don't like bullies and I don't take shit.' I think it's been a steady progression of not putting up with a lot of things.

I think, as a mother, if I had a nine-year-old, I would tell my daughter not to do that, but on the inside, I'd be like, 'YES!'

I don't even think I told my parents. I think I just did it. I can still remember his face and how shocked he was. I didn't slap him hard; I just remember thinking, 'I'm not putting up with anymore of this, Nathan Wilson!'

What is Julie's definition of the female entrepreneur?

Someone who has decided to buck the system. There's a certain amount in not playing by someone else's rules. And there's an amount of, 'I know that I can do this, and I'm going to try.' The good female entrepreneurs, we're really fortunate that, as women, we can ask for help sometimes—at least I can. I have had the ability to ask for help where men a lot of times aren't raised to ask for help. Women have been so good at supporting each other, even though we've been raised in a new generation where all boats rise with the tides, right? There's this new generation where we're not competing for that. It's someone who's chosen to say, 'I'm going to be a part of this. I see something that needs a solution and I'm going to do whatever I have to do to make that happen.' Whether it's an internal solution, like making money for my family and still being able to take care of my children, or whether it's an external solution, like Sarah Blakely and needing something to wear under white pants! She's amazing; I just love her so much.

It is someone who has seen the odds because they are not necessarily in our favor: we don't get the money that men get. They're a good female entrepreneur because they have seen the odds, and they are going to do it anyway.

It's betting on yourself.

100%.

It's rolling the dice, knowing you are taking that chance, whether you hit those numbers or not.

I think so many female entrepreneurs have been told no so many times in the system, that they're like, 'Screw it.' It's like me and when the company I wanted to work for didn't exist.

So, you created it.

And so, I built it.

I really resonate with your verbiage on that and saying, 'buck the system.' I remember thinking back to my corporate days when I was doing PR. The first recession had hit, and our CEO at the time was not a good person. I remember thinking on my way out the door that day, 'I am going to do something where nobody has that kind of control over me.' A lot of us can relate, and I still think there's women sitting in these cubicles that are thinking, 'I don't know how to get out.'

100%. 100%.

Last question. Complete this sentence… What if I….

What if I could be happy every day for the rest of my life? Here's the thing, I am happy every day. It goes back to one of your other questions in that it's gratitude. I find one of my superpowers is the ability to find the silver lining in everything. So, I find that silver lining in everything because I believe everything that happens, even the worst things, are for the good eventually. If you can turn your life around and find a way to be happy even after all the left-turn horrendous mistakes…

I have a husband and a beautiful daughter and a life that I love, working with people that I love, doing a job that I love. So, what if you could be happy every day? I don't mean every second, every minute—blissfully unaware all day every day. That's just unrealistic. But what if you could find the silver lining in even the worst of things?

My husband, who is always touring, was no longer on the road during the pandemic. For me, the bright spot was my husband got to spend tons of time with Roxy. He had been on tour most of the year before and was traveling eight months out of the year give or take. He and Roxy got to be just best friends this last summer, and it was great.

That was beautiful for you to watch, I bet.

100%. It was hard; I didn't leave the house for three months at a time. But again, what if I could be happy for at least one minute every day for the rest of my life?

Here's the magical thing about that: we get to choose.

The number one trait of happy people is gratitude. So, if you come into your life with that every single day…if you can find those times, and it brings in that moment of gratitude and you say that prayer, 'Thank you for my family, thank you for my food, thank you for taking care of us today…' When you come into your life with that attitude, it's that idea of your have-tos get to become get-tos. For example, I have so much work to do I have a job, I have so much laundry to do; I have clothes on my back, all of those things. And if you can approach everything from that standpoint, your life gets so much better, and you become such a happier person.

COME SWEAT OR SILT

Meet Callie Katz, the author who listened to her gut when the stakes were high. The podcast host for Sweat or Silt, giving female entrepreneurs a platform to share their epic journeys and excels at creating elite partnerships as the CEO of Luxe + Lush, a public relations company.

Truth be told, I didn't want to write this chapter. I was more than willing to showcase yet another amazing leader. I guess that's what we do when we deflect. However, I realized that *Come Sweat or Silt* has been the ultimate sacrifice of what I have experienced and given up in the years leading up to becoming a female entrepreneur myself.

I know now more than ever that this book was supposed to be here. To be a platform for women across the globe to share their stories of guilt, sadness, successes, and the real, raw truth of what this journey takes.

It is also a testament to the many years I have spent climbing my own mountain, walking through the valleys of pain and heartache as I kept pursuing the silent voice inside of me that told me I was made for so much more.

So, let me ask you this. How far are you willing to climb?

△ △ △

As a young child, I knew I had a gift. I practically taught myself how to read (kudos to *Sesame Street*), wrote above average, never studied for a spelling test, and could be found in my "office" sitting on an Osh-Kosh plastic chair, hidden behind a tainted yellow accent piece surrounded by 1980s wooden

bookshelves. If you asked me what I wanted to be when I grew up, I would respond, "a famous author."

Fast forward decades later, life and adulting kicked in. I was bringing home the bacon in the form of an 80-hour work week, serving multi-millionaires across professional sports leagues, acting as their PR guru. Sound fancy? Allow me to give you some insight…

If there was one thing I knew early on in my career, it was that I never wanted to be "stuck." I wanted to make sure I was going somewhere big. After graduating from college on a Friday, I began work for my hometown's NFL team that following Monday.

I thought I had hit the jackpot! Here I was stepping onto a field where champions were made, legacies were created, and the principal founder of today's beloved sport had borne his household name. I knew from day one I wanted to be a part of that team's history.

There are often times I reflect back to my seasons spent as a rookie in those offices. Even after I left, I had a hard time watching the game of football as a fan again. I would look at everything from a business lens and break down each sector. But the one thing that stands out to me the most during that time is the people I was surrounded by.

It wasn't hard for me to determine who was going to make a difference in the role I played. I quickly figured out who was who, their roles, and which relationships I could trust. The words of my first mentor in the sports world still play a reel in my head after all these years. "Make it a great day," he would say. Gary Spani, a former NFL linebacker and Hall of Fame inductee, helped educate me on the brand, the working parts of how an NFL team operated, and how to run special events and partnerships. I was hooked!

The following season, the offices started making shifts. Roles were changing, new leadership stepped in, and for the first time, I was unsure of where I was going in the company. I wasn't excited about it. My new role now fell under a female director that taught me one of the biggest life lessons I would learn in my young career.

I felt like I had been demoted. My tasks no longer excited me, and there was a control over me that made me feel uneasy. I had become her "Girl Friday." I felt like I was seeking constant approval on a daily basis. I knew I had to find a way out. I so badly wanted to stay with the organization, just not in the department I was currently working in. I started looking around the offices to see if other departments were hiring and caught wind that there was an open position down the hallway. It wasn't my first pick, but it was something else—that's all I needed. As I interviewed for the new role, I remember feeling like I wanted to plead, asking the director to please, please let me transfer. However, I knew I had to stay professional.

In the days after the interview, my current boss was told that I had looked into another department. She pulled me into her office for a meeting. As she began to speak to me, I honestly thought she was in my corner. I thought, *this isn't so bad, she wants me to succeed and climb the ladder here*. This was my chance!

I wasn't prepared for the words I would hear next. I was told that if I EVER looked for another job within the organization again, I would be let go, and the role I currently filled was the only role I would ever succumb to.

IT WAS NOT A GREAT DAY.

The writing was on the wall. On the inside, I was in the fetal position, crying, because I knew I could not do this to myself. I couldn't settle. I had much, much bigger visions and standards, and shutting those down were not an option.

On my last day, I walked into my mentor's office with tears. I knew I wasn't going to see him again for a very long time. I had thought of him like family—truth be told, he was a little like family, as I found out later that the godmother to his children was my grandmother's best friend! I knew he was good people!

I continued in the sports industry and left for another arena, Major League Soccer. Let's just say one season was enough. I wasn't a fan of the sport, never watched it on a professional level, and the only reason I took the job was because I knew familiar faces.

Ladies, listen to your gut, and if it's not a *HELL YES*, DON'T DO IT!

I came on board in hopes that I would be walking into a better position than what I had left. It was here that I truly learned what the definition of "smoke and mirrors" meant. I also learned that when others dream big, they are not dreaming for you, they are dreaming for themselves.

There were so many promises. So many big-picture moments that were supposed to happen, but never did. I began to feel distorted. I even questioned what my actual title was and the work I was supposed to be doing. What was I doing here? There were a lot of days where I found myself literally watching the clock! Daydreaming about leaving the luxuries of an office cubicle, and here I was!

That is when the rumors started to fly! Doors were being shut, conversations became "hush-hush," and I knew something was going on. My gut told me it was something I didn't want to be a part of.

I was right—and, in bold print, distributed all across the city—that's how I found out. The rumors I had heard had been true. The behaviors of those I was supposed to take the lead from absolutely disgusted me. Local reporters had done their due diligence and began calling every female staff member for comment. I remember telling my parents not to answer the phone from the media. It was the last thing I EVER wanted to be involved with. In fact, I was sitting at my desk one day when a television crew walked into the front doors ready to pounce! They were quickly escorted out, and next I knew, we had security. We were all trained on what we could say and what not to say, should similar events happen again.

I was in the middle of a tornado and didn't have any part in bringing this storm.

That sinking feeling in my stomach had resurfaced, telling me it was time to go again. I remember sitting down in a colleague's office, asking him for advice. This was someone I knew I could trust; he was a good family man, and we had come from the same arena in the working world. His advice to me: "Callie, you need to get out."

Then, I got the call. I happened to answer the main line when I heard a familiar voice over the phone asking if Callie was available. Hell yes I was! I walked out of the office to take the call on my cell phone and was offered an interview for another opportunity in a different sports arena!

Allow me to time travel for a minute. As a college student, I was very driven when it came to my post-grad career, and as I mentioned earlier, I wanted to go straight to the top! Even amidst taking classes, sorority activities, and landing multiple internships, I was always connecting for my future and nurtured those relationships. This is where that call had come from.

After the interview, I felt excited again. That feeling that I thought I had lost was now back, and I knew I wanted this job more than ever (or so I thought). I even had custom cookies made with the brand's colors and had them sent to those who had interviewed me. Pretty good, right?

Well, those cookies must have been damn good because I got the job! I was acting as a PR consultant for a race team in several different series, writing releases for numerous publications, landing MAJOR spots in media outlets for our clients, the list goes on. However, as my team and I worked race weekend after race weekend, we began to notice the grueling work environment we were a part of. This wasn't just your average "hard days" kind of work. This became demanding 100-hour weeks, and it wasn't healthy. To the point where I would lie awake at night waiting for the three-a.m. approval that something needed to be sent out or done ASAP. I was losing sleep and barely eating because I would feel physically sick, anxiously awaiting what would happen next.

When I hear stories about "bad bosses," I almost find it humorous. Sadly, I've rarely heard a story that blows mine out of the water. I don't mean to degrade anyone's feelings based on their personal experiences; however, when you are being verbally abused on a daily basis (enough to get legal involved) and feel physically sick driving up to work because you don't know what's going to happen to you that day, it becomes a different ball game. In fact, for the longest time after I left that job, I wouldn't even be able to drive by that building because I would feel like I was going to throw up, or I would start shaking.

I really knew how to pick em, eh?

As time went on, my team and I noticed other pieces that didn't add up for the type of work we were doing. The way accounts were being set up, new partnerships were created, ensuring our main client (and backer) always had videos, press releases, and special events hosted where others were rarely involved. There was one time when my director and I went to the offices of our main client, and the offices were unmarked. When we found the department, it was labeled with initials that looked vaguely familiar from other accounts we had seen on paper. It didn't take long to put those pieces together. This was a dirty operation! It wasn't just time to find a better job, it was time to get the hell out before I became a part of something that was beyond the power of little old me.

The law stepped in next. The local police department became VIP members, visiting the offices on a weekly basis. I noticed that every time they came in, they always held an envelope in their hands. I wanted to do something so badly to help them out and stick it to the man upstairs. I even contemplated pulling one of the officers out into the hallway to tell them that who they were looking for was just down the hall, 20 yards away, and he wasn't "out of the country" as they were being told. Do you really think no one's heard that before? It would be like watching an episode of *The Price is Right* and the contestant opens Door Number Two! Tell them what they've won, Bob! HA!

However, I let both my fear and dignity get in the way. Maybe that was a good thing. I wanted to leave on a clean slate, get out of dodge, and never look back—and I wanted my name erased from it.

The hardest part in looking for a new job was that a recession had hit. Unfortunately, my area of expertise wasn't a high recruiting role at the time. I looked for over a year and can still remember the hours I spent contacting old colleagues, friends of friends, conducting Indeed and LinkedIn searches. With each day that went by, I became border-line depressed. My director had left because it was too much for him, and I knew the day he did, I was screwed because he was the semi-shelter between myself and the man that owned the company.

I no longer had the smallest bit of protection. I was already a target before, but now it was open season! I was the sole 8-point buck in an abandoned field.

One weekend, I was capturing yet another race (I was not present as per usual). That's how we worked: The PR consultant didn't go to the events! I had to phone in to find out what had happened from various members of the crew while watching a small tracker on my computer back at home. That was a task in and of itself. We had all worked close to a 30-hour weekend when Monday morning came around. I remember getting the video from the photography team, writing out stats and highlights from the event, and launching the press release on our site prior to the lunch hour. What happened next, I will never forget.

The BOSS's right-hand woman came to my desk and retrieved me. I walked back with her to the conference room and sat down. There was no hesitation in her delivery. I was being let go. I had worked an entire weekend, burning the midnight oil, and had given everything I could. WTF?! I realized he waited until Monday on purpose, wanting to milk me for one last event. Yet, the boss didn't have the balls to do it himself. Truth be told, HR didn't even do the job.

You would think I would have been emotional, but I wasn't. I was the opposite. I found myself "faking" my reaction, asking if I had done anything wrong? On the inside, I was only slightly disappointed I wasn't walking away on my own terms. That's what really stung. I knew I hadn't done anything wrong; I did the job thoroughly because I was so scared. There had been a pattern of people being let go in our offices based on his mood that day, and I was next on the list because I had stood up for myself in one of my emails I had sent over the weekend.

Next thing I knew, I was being walked out to my car in the parking lot, acting stunned along the way. I had wanted to leave for so long I didn't even have personal items to bring home as I had cleared house months ago. I even took it as far as clearing files.

As I sat in my car, I realized I didn't even know where to go, and at the time, home was only ten minutes away. I immediately called my father and told him what had happened. His next words were priceless. He told me to come over to their house and that we were going to celebrate with margaritas! We sure did! I was free! Tears started running down my face uncontrollably because I knew I no longer had to feel the pain, the sickness, and the anxiety I had felt nearly every day for two years. I had worked for a conman, and I believed in karma.

The next morning, I filed for unemployment. It was accepted in less than 24 hours.

I was unemployed for nearly two years! I don't wish this upon ANYONE! The recession had hit so hard, and no one was hiring. There were only so many hours in the day that I could sit at the computer and search for jobs. I even found myself making ruthless task lists around my apartment, and because the money from the government wasn't too hot, I couldn't just jump in the car all the time and drive for hours. I had to factor in gas and how much time errands would take: would it get me to next week, etc.? I even had to ask my parents for help, and it made me feel like I had failed. I found creative ways to do "free" things! There was a high school up the street from where I lived. I had been athletic most of my life and thought, *Let's take it back to the good ol' days and get up in the wee hours of the morning to go run the track or do stairs.* So, that's what I did! It helped me take up morning time, which ultimately led to nighttime so I could go back to bed!

It became a habit. Once I got into the groove, I realized it was also helping me burn much-needed energy from sitting at home. Not to mention the health benefits! Months after I started this routine, I realized once a day wasn't killing enough time, so I began to work out twice a day.

I was getting back into fitness and joined a boot camp class. In the process, I found myself being mentored by a friend that helped me get through those days of unemployment. One day, he asked me if I had ever thought about running my own business—this way I wouldn't be waiting on someone to give me a job! LIGHTBULB!

I had never thought I would run my own business! I had dreams of directing PR in the sports world and was still set on doing that. However, his words lit something in me. I was intrigued as to what this could look like. He had run his own business for years, and I loved the way his schedule worked. Why would I hold myself back from being able to do the same thing? If I had my own business, I would never be let go again, nor would a corporation determine my destiny!

I was SOLD! Collectively, my corporate experiences had placed me in the most noted arenas across the globe, and I had met some amazing people that taught me so much at the start of my career. However, I had also experienced some harsh life lessons, ones I never want to return to, and yet, it is why I have built such thick skin over the years. Needless to say, I don't have a tolerance for bullshit nor people who bully others into getting what they want. I will cut that cord in a second!

What I didn't know when I made the decision to be an entrepreneur was all the trials and tribulations that would be ahead of me. This is one hell of a rollercoaster, and you better be ready for the ride!

This takes grit! And, if you've read this far, you know that already. My journey is *COME SWEAT OR SILT.* It has defined my entire career, both in corporate and out. Nothing comes without a price. I have been an entrepreneur for nearly two decade now. Yes, it's hard. Yes, I have broken down after being tested, time and time again. But if there is one thing I know, I have one hell of an inner fight in me. And that CANNOT be taken away. It's what has pushed me to keep going on the days I've wanted to give up on myself. But had I done that, I wouldn't be where I am today. And although it may sound cliche, it's true. This journey has opened me in so many ways. It has taught me who I want in my corner, where I'm willing to draw the line for myself and my family, and that there are opportunities in front of me that I cannot even see yet. When you leave it out all on the table, good things come. I am still making connections that I would never have expected. I am still opening my arms to new people and new friends in my life. And I am still being coached by some of the greatest women I have ever known, ones that are and will continue to be an integral part of this journey. I was ready to write my own rules, I just didn't know if I was ready to follow.

Sink or swim, you will get told, "NO," but what will you do with it? I will rise and conquer above all challenges because that is who I am and will always have skin in the game. Today, I am on a mission to create exponential growth, allowing radical renovation while ultimately leaving a legacy. Because I played with the scary AF yeses, I am owning the truth into who I really came here to be.

Bet on yourself and roll the dice. You may just hit the jackpot after all.

> "Bet on yourself and roll the dice. You may just hit the jackpot after all..."
> — Callie Katz

TRAINING FOR LIFE

Meet Eve Overland-Owner of Eve Overland Fitness, fit52 Collaborator, and the Ultimate Road Warrior!

Motion is her birthright. A former dancer, competitor in bodybuilding, figure, powerlifting + CrossFit, not to mention lighting herself on fire as a stuntwoman and working as a professional actor, Eve Overland has always been one for forward movement. And it's never stopped. Her resume is a force to be reckoned with. Known to many for her work as a personal trainer for music superstar Carrie Underwood, Overland has been recognized for her own artistry in the world of fitness.

But it's the passion for her people and vice versa, that has earned her more than the title of personal trainer and fitness instructor. Over the last two years, I have had the pleasure of sharing stories, laughs, and moments of tenacity that have cleared the path to where she is today. So, allow me to let this Atlanta gal tell you, her path.

△ △ △

CK: How did you start shaping yourself for entrepreneurship?

EO: *I didn't, ever. This was not something I was intentionally doing or knew I had to do. My entire life I've always worked for myself. I've always been essentially my own boss.*

My degree was in theater and dance. When you ask that question, I'm like, "I'm not an entrepreneur." But, as an actor, a performer, and having worked in casting, and teaching group fitness, I've been my own thing. I guess I never thought about being my own business back then (this was in the 90s). It's amazing how things evolve and change and morph, and here I am 20 years later not doing anything I studied. However, every little piece of my journey has landed me to owning my own business, Eve Overland Fitness.

It was a natural progression for me to become a personal trainer. Yet, how I landed in the online business was out of necessity per se. In 2014, I felt a shift in where group fitness and personal training was going. I remember getting introduced to Peloton and things were kind of moving away from Eve coming to Callie's house for an hour and expanding to more of an OnDemand streaming or app situation.

It was then that I moved from Nashville to Atlanta thinking I would rekindle my stunt career as a 40-year-old. Things hurt a lot more when you are 40 (LAUGHS). I didn't have any personal training clients; I just literally up and moved. In fact, I couldn't even get a job waitressing! I was broke and had made this move to change my life and career. I knew online training was a thing, so I reached out to some friends about how I could promote myself and services. Prior to moving, I had also lived in Los Angeles for 10 years. I would drive an hour plus to get to a client and still only get to charge for that hour. The question was, how can I make this more efficient and help more people? So, I started online training.

I had to make money because (obviously) I couldn't live without it. I don't want this audience to feel like they need to be an entrepreneur because of desperation or money; however, sometimes that's when you are the most creative.

It was like having a little voice inside my head saying I got this. The wheels started spinning, allowing me to figure out how to make this all happen. Did my online business grow fast? No. Is it still growing? Yes. So, it is still a constant evolution. It is still trying to see where the fitness industry is going. Is it more OnDemand, is it more apps, is it more MIRRORs (Interactive On Demand Fitness Device)? I have no idea how I landed here, just with one foot in front of the other.

When I did take action, I didn't force it. By doing this, I was able to see clearer, things just kind of landed in a way that wasn't forced. Do I have a bazillion dollars?

Absolutely not. Am I still working quite a bit for even just a basic day? Yes. But if you don't force it, I think that's where the journey is amazing, and you just let it happen. I'm not saying don't take action; be productive, but just don't force anything.

CK: When you are open to it, opportunities come. When you're forcing yourself and stressing out over x, y and z all day long, it's almost resisting what could be coming to you. I can relate when you say you don't want people to get to that desperation point for entrepreneurship to happen. I was in a similar situation. I was out of corporate and had been laid off; that's part of my story along with everybody else in the recession around 2010. I really had to decide what to do because my industry was not hiring at the time. I needed to make money and filing for unemployment for two years was not going to be an option.

EO: Absolutely. Yes, it becomes a necessity, but it also gets you in a creative mindset or gets you thinking outside the box. You're never too young or too old to reinvent yourself. But you're not even reinventing yourself, you're just building and growing. As humans, we are not stagnant, we're always changing. So why not in career? Why not once you've put yourself in a box (if that's where you're comfortable), think about what could be by just trusting and allowing the evolution of your life.

CK: I talk to people about this all the time. I have a thing where I say, what if? I even talk to my stepdaughters about it. What if you didn't go back to school this year? You wouldn't have found the new boyfriend in the first two weeks of school, lol, and it's just one of those things. Stop doubting yourself and start asking yourself, what if this could really happen? You don't know where the road is going to take you.

EO: Right. And it may take you eight other careers to land here. And it did for me. I've had so many jobs and so many careers, so many paths I've taken. They all married themselves into my business. Everything I've done from performing to casting has landed me into online training. But it's interesting because I'm not staying here. What I'm doing right now just in this industry is constantly growing and evolving. You have to really stay ahead of the game. To be relevant, you have to be open to change and to be pivoting. Don't get too married to what is trending right now because guess what? Tomorrow is fall fashion and then it's going to be winter fashion.

It's like when you go to the stores and it's Halloween and Christmas is already out.

I can't take it. For me, Christmas is like one week before.

One holiday at a time.

I joke because, as entrepreneurs, if you looked at all of our resumes, it would look like none of us could hold a job.

That's funny you say that because I could not get a job after I had moved. Today, I am a celebrity personal trainer, but eight years prior to that, I couldn't even find a waitressing job. I was overqualified for a lot of things. Then, my credit cards were maxed out, I was borrowing money from my parents, and was freaking out. But it was the best idea to make this move, and this is where I am, and I love it. I've planted my roots here in Georgia. I'd like to see our resumes…it's like we've been fired from every job. We are Jack of all trades.

How did we do it? I wouldn't trade any of it. I'm at the point where I feel confident and grounded, and I think that's what I've always wanted. I work in a very influx industry, but to have that anchor to grow from, that's what Atlanta or this area did for me. It gave me an anchor, like I feel like I'm going to stay here. It only took 43 years… to get here.

But you made it.

You're never too old.

It is those sink or swim moments and making that decision to jump that ship. It wasn't exactly the moment of desperation we all hoped for, but *I'm either going to bet on myself or let somebody else bet for me.*

I love hearing you say you wouldn't change it because it's gotten you where you are today. But, if there were anything in the last decade, would there be anything you would change?

Yes and no. Was it ugly and messy, awful and depressing, and were there the lowest of lows of my life…absolutely. Do you know what I mean? Once you feel that low or that defeated and deflated, you have the ability to come out the other side and your body responds to that. It understands that pain and it also understands that it will go away. Your body reacts to stress. Anything can be a stressor: mentally, emotionally, financially, but would I change it? Probably not. There were a lot of things I would have liked to do or know. I wish I would have known a lot of basic things in a business sense. I couldn't sell cookies as a Girl Scout. HA!

*Know your worth. What I didn't know and what I still have problems with is charging. I still feel very anxious, like apologetic. I am a service, a premier service. What am I worth? A lot of people don't want to pay what you charge, so then you think people **can't,** but I really need money. For some business owners it might not be that way, but for me it was very difficult to charge and still is.*

One more thing. One of the biggest industries to ever evolve and change is technology. We didn't have the foresight at the time to know it would essentially become our business card with social media. To know where social media was going in the forms of advertisement, I wish I would have paid more attention that way. On the contrary, what you and I both have is the ability to talk to humans. For example, I found you and you found me by referral. It's knowing and trusting by referral, rather than scrolling and saying, 'Her arms look great, I want to meet her!" We weren't forced to create, we just did and had natural networking. I know there is social media networking, but it is different than actually meeting a human being or having a referral. And that's actually how I got the BIG job with my current client! Even though it was through referral, I still was hired on my own merit. If I wasn't who I was and worked as hard as I had then, the stars wouldn't have aligned for this 'somebody who knew somebody.' In essence, we have to have better personal social skills.

It forces you to up level yourself in another area. I was talking with a potential client of mine, and he asked, "How are you going to help me find sponsorships for our celebrity-status projects?" I responded that I had my connections and let me do that for you. I didn't want him sending out a letter, hoping the right

person received it. Those letters don't get read. Everyone gets fed so much all day long.

Right. So, I think maybe that's a good point to throw in there about genuine human connection. Don't lose that in your hustle. Even though we're all on our phones, people can still read a room. They can feel like you're the kind of person that is sincere. You can also feel it when you meet those people who are in it for more selfish reasons. It's like, "I want to get to know Callie because what can she do for ME?" I feel like where the real success and the growth happens is with being honest and having to meet people authentically, rather than expecting them to give you something. That's when people want to hire you.

It's not just a business one-off (you win, I win, great). Those long-term partnerships are the ones that do help elevate you, and you may only have this person in that space for a certain service or time, but then down the road, you may end up reconnecting again because you've kept that person in your realm.

You've grown from group fitness instructor to training clients one-on-one; what works best for you? Do you like the combination of both, or do you prefer traveling for sessions?

It is interesting because, as a personal trainer, you cannot NOT be personal. Another struggle creating an online business is to have a personal connection with somebody via email. Do I love what I'm doing? Yes, I love my people. But I don't take a lot of clients because I would have guilt not giving as much service as I would be giving if I were to come to your house and train you in person.

There's a ton of different ways to online train, and there's a lot of awesome online trainers who have people that work under them, or they have a way better organized or automated situation than I do. But, I grow, and I thrive working best with people. I work better in partnerships, feeding off of their energy, seeing people during group fitness or live events, even virtual events where I am able to talk to people. It's not scalable. I always cap my number of clients because I want to know that they're okay, but that's just me. It depends on what the client needs, what they expect, and if you're a premium service, I want to deliver that. How can I scale that, again, to touch more people and how can I do it in a way that fills me? Having kept the same clients anywhere from five years plus, you know you're doing something right.

So, to take all of this kinetic energy and to put it into online, that is a challenge for me. I love my clients and I love creating content, but what is tough for me is to sit down, put it, plug it, and play it.

Time management is also a tough one. Everything shifted in 2020, and I've never been the kind of person (being such a mover) to sit and bullet point journal; I wish I was. But then I wouldn't be me. I wish I had the discipline to create social media content M/W/F from 8-10am, and then read a gratitude journal and do all the things Mel Robbins tells you to do! For example, the 4-Hour Work Week and all those self-help books. I tried! If it doesn't feel good to me, I just never do it. So, time management, organization, learning media, knowing how to do all the sales, MailChimp's, funnels…I just want to be a creator. I know this may sound cliche, but I am an artist, I am a dancer, I am creatively sculpting the workouts. I cannot help not to have a flow to my workouts. It's like a story with a middle and an end.

My clients may want to achieve a certain physique goal, so when I look at them, I think, how can I help this person do that? If everything else is on point, how can I help sculpt this body?

Part of this book is to help us see the lessons in how to eliminate the guesswork no matter where we are in our businesses. Even if we're in the middle of it, we're still evolving, we're still growing, and at some point, you know you can't do this alone. You just can't. Because if you do, you could be wasting thousands and thousands of dollars of your own money.

Know and outsource if you can. I actually hired my own business coach who I love, (I'll plug her) Kourtney Thomas. I don't even think she's even business coaching anymore as she has parlayed her career into a global femme empire. I found her on a podcast and cold called her. She was a trainer at the time, and I said I needed help. She helped me build my website and advised me in strategy.

Was that a big investment? For me at that time. I did not have a lot of money. Was it 100% worth it? Absolutely. It's hard to throw money at the front end; sometimes you do, and you cross your fingers hoping that it will pan out. I've been very lucky. It takes money to make money, ya know?

Bottom line, know when to invest and be confident. If it doesn't pan out, don't beat yourself up. It's all a learning experience. I might have asked for help sooner, but I felt like it came at a good time because it was right when I was moving my business online in 2014.

When your clients ask for help and invest in you in return it's not just a matter of them thinking I can't do this without Eve, they are investing in you as a person. We can all go do something on a treadmill or lift some weights at one point or another; whether they do it correctly or not, that's another game, but it's because they want you in their lives.

And I do them. Keeping that core group. I always say call me or text me whenever, but that's not scalable if you have hundreds of clients. Moving to a more subscription-based platform is where I see fitness has been going or is. To the Pelotons, to the MIRRORs, and coming out of necessity, virtual Zoom situations. There's been quite a few software developments that can give trainers their own platforms or webinars where you can sign up for a class for live group fitness streaming.

You've been inching yourself into that realm. You have a partnership with Carrie Underwood's fit52 app where people do buy a subscription service. Tell us about your collaboration with it and what is your role in setting those workouts up?

Eve Overland Fitness and fit52 are different from each other. it52 is our baby. It is based on a fitness game that has been around forever, based on a card game. There are 52 cards in a deck and there are four different suits. Each suit represents a body part/exercise and then the number you draw is the number of reps that you perform. Carrie loved it. She likes numbers; she's a numbers person. She has always loved the game. That was one of the first workouts she and I ever did together. It's not because it's mind blowing, but it's fun, interactive, creative, and it stuck with her. Really what I do with Carrie, and the team behind the fit52 app, is to help develop the content creation. This means curating the various exercises in the app for beginners, intermediate, and advanced, which are constantly evolving and being updated. It's never doing the same workout twice. It challenges the users with new exercises, hitting different muscle groups with a new challenge each time. You never know what you're going to get and in what order.

When you train your clients, you're helping give them more energy in their day-to-day, pushing their bodies to a new level, but what do you do for you? How do you recharge? Is that going for a run with the dog? Is that spending some R&R time for yourself?

I recharge with movement as a creative expression. I run with the dog every day, that's a no brainer. Getting outside in nature is important to me; my head isn't right if I don't. I take a lot of naps, not gonna lie. I also recharge with conversations like this. Having an in-depth conversation about 'how did you get here?' or 'how do you feel?' and have the space to answer something other than 'I'm good.' I get excited learning from other people and if I can help in any way in having that common mutual exchange in skill set (I guess that's why partnerships are so great), we're sharing information. Your whole process with this book definitely sparks creativity just in my journey. To sum it up, talking to people like you, being in nature, I love theater, I love dance, and I nap. If you're an entrepreneur and you work for yourself, just don't hit that snooze! (LAUGHS)

You can take that nap anytime you want!

Thatta girl. Why do we want to be entrepreneurs? Just so we can nap anytime we want.

Nobody can tell us no. LOL.

Use three words to describe yourself; what would they be?

I love this question. I would say creative, kinetic, and tough. Creative and kinetic are who I am. My mom would call me witty; my dad would call me a pistol; my clients might call me a badass or sister. But who am I as a businesswoman? Yes, still creative, and kinetic. But really who am I? I would say loyal. I hope to be authentic and have integrity, I guess that's why I've kept my clients for so long. Your personality and your business don't have to be separate. If you're your own business, it's your heart, it's your soul, it's you.

I love that you put tough in there. As a business owner, you develop your own brand of true grit along the way. You don't just jump into this tribe because anybody can do it. It takes a certain amount of grit to be an entrepreneur, and you're in here for a reason. Whether you knew it at the beginning or not, you are.

It does take true grit. It takes balls; it takes risk. And some people aren't risk takers, but I've always kind of gone for it.

It's the stunt woman in ya!

I've always gone for the back flips. I will always take those calculated risks. Even growing up in theater and trying out for commercials and TV, sometimes you don't get the job. And it can be because of how you look or how you talk. I've been a fitness competitor and judges are looking at your body and sometimes they do not like you. It's easy to get down on yourself (whether I didn't get the part, or I wasn't a good enough actor or didn't come out with the best physique in a competition). It can just smash your freaking soul. You just need to know it's really not about you. Just keep going and know that you can move forward. If I could give advice, I wish people weren't so hard on themselves and didn't doubt themselves. Because I spent a crap ton of years doubting, hating, putting myself down…it was exhausting.

It is. It's more mentally tough on your body than having a sore muscle.

I don't know when things start to shift. I hope people don't wait until they're in their 40s..my shift was my perfect timing. I just let it go. My world opened up when I didn't give a shit anymore, you know? I don't care about needing to have 'x' number of posts or I have to have all this money and be bigger in my career. Could I be? Sure. But I'm going to do it my way and in a way that feels good to me. I would tell your people don't sell yourself short, but don't sell yourself out. Maybe that's why I'm not bigger. I'm not going to take advantage of anybody and just do it my way.

What is the legacy you want to leave behind?

That's a great question. I hope that I've done a good job in my life and career. I just want to be remembered, and I think I will. Maybe not by the world, but a lot of people that matter to me. My legacy may end up being the crazy cat lady, who knows? (LAUGHS).

At the end of the day, you want to be known for you. Who you were as a person. And that's all that should matter. It's your inner circle, who you are to them and vice versa.

I know that sounds kind of cliche, and I wish I had more of a poignant answer.

I guess the answer is simple when it really comes down to it. We're all really crazy and complex.

I'm also grateful that I'm not in a place where I'm financially insecure. I know that sounds scary, but that's a reality for a lot of people. Money is what allows us to live, daily costs, work life, through recessions and pandemics, etc.

And you were able to keep going with your business that year.

You as well. We are some of the people that got lucky. I'm grateful for opportunities like this one. People like you call me out of the blue and say hey, I think you'd be a good fit. It makes me feel like I'm doing something right when somebody wants to know my story or wants my help. They think I have something valuable to provide. What I'm doing is obviously working somehow and I can be trusted not just as an expert in my field, but also as a trusted friend. Trust is important, especially in working with high profile people. I'm super grateful that I get to tour and travel for a living. Even though I keep myself busy with the shows, I'm so lucky that my job allows me to take a walk in the town that I'm in. I actually get to explore. You're only around one time, might as well see what you can!

Lastly, if there were any advice I could give, it would be to not be paralyzed by perfection. I could have started a Netflix type subscription and had a more passive

> *"Don't be paralyzed into wanting it to be all perfect."*
> *Eve Overland*

stream of income, but I didn't. I was worried about the production value or having the right cameras, and I want things to look good. People aren't looking at your background. They just want to know your workout. Don't be paralyzed by wanting it to be all perfect. I still struggle with that. Just get it out there. Be authentic. People want to know what makes you human and not just a pre-manipulated somebody on Instagram, ya know?

I'M CALLING BS

ALLERGIC TO PERFECT

Ditch the doubt. Ditch the perfectionism, and definitely ditch the social media highlight reels.

Meet Nat Tolhopf, New Zealand-based author and one badass business coach.

After a sudden health crisis, she realized she had been building her business in all the wrong ways. It wasn't until she decided to let go of the social BS, drop the self-sabotage, and trust her instincts that she then cracked the code to six-figure status.

So, pull up the big girl pants, get in check, and get ready to listen to the hard truth!

△   △   △

NT: *I used to be a massive perfectionist. By trade, I'm a trained chef, so naturally precision trained. You can't have an element of imperfection when you're cooking. So, when I started my own business, I came with this perfectionist attitude and discipline. It actually stopped me in my tracks. That brought about self-doubt, worry, sabotage, imposter syndrome, and I didn't know what to do. A coach helped me normalize that. It's normal to feel doubt, overwhelm, all those things. They don't actually ever go away; you just learn to ride through them and make them part of who you are. That's how I've become the opposite to what I was.*

My story and success come from my own imperfect tapestry of life. I had gone overseas as a chef, then came back to New Zealand owning my bravado and ego and decided to open up my own restaurant in a new partnership. We crashed and burned! We didn't pay our taxes because we bought new furniture to look good. In the meantime, we couldn't even pay ourselves nor our rent. The rats were jumping out of our ship because we were sinking it. So, for me, I really learned business from doing it wrong and all the failures we had. That's my university diploma in what not to do!

From there, I became a business consultant for other hospitality owners. Because I had been there, I knew how to guide them. I loved training the young staff we had, and so I went and became a tutor. I was able to teach hospitality management to students through real life scenarios.

This is when it gets weird! I'm in this private school teaching and the management owners tell me we are going through a massive change and think I should be the next leader to run this business!

I was now a general manager of a seven-million-dollar business. It was the best and hardest thing I've ever done in my life. When I stepped into leadership, I saw my strengths and where I had gone wrong on my last business. At the time I was promoted, I had a one-year-old baby and another child down the line. I was traveling, working so many hours, the money was amazing, but I knew I was here for so much more. I think for high achievers, we often know that in our gut. We are here to serve and make an impact; it's something you can't take away. That's when I decided to stick it to the business and left.

This time, Facebook was relatively new, and I decided to start an online business. That didn't work out either. I crashed and burned AGAIN! Having these failures were really strengthening my success muscle. It was during this phase that people really began to see me in a leadership position. They loved my energy, and I had women asking me if I would help mentor them.

But here's where imposter syndrome came in. I told them I was riddled with failures. However, they responded that I was a success in teaching because I could say what not to do.

I decided to ditch my perfectionism! My first business had been built on fancy websites, photos; everything looked perfect, but it wasn't making me any money.

The business I have now, I just decided to put it out there. Imperfections and all (without looking unprofessional). I knew how to solve problems to the right market. I stepped into a simple 1:1 business and it's grown from there. Five years later, and here we are today.

CK: **How are you working with your audience today?**

NT: *I primarily help women sell with confidence. How I do that is getting them to take imperfect actions. Drop the doubt, embrace all of who you are; the strategies and tactics change all the time.*

CK: **What I think we can most relate with is you mentioned having that sinking feeling of knowing you were meant for more but you can't explain it.**

I've had that feeling since I was a kid. And, like you, I know I was meant for something bigger! It's not that my family didn't show me more, they only showed me what they knew. And I couldn't ever explain it. Still to this day, that gut feeling has stayed with me, and I truly think that this book is part of the plan.

You talk about feeling trapped, but at what point did you jump all in and say I believe in myself? What made you do that?

NT: I was looking at other people who were my friends creating success, placing them on a pedestal. I became crazy obsessed with, what's the difference between them and me? It was just the self-belief. That there was no difference. They were just taking more action and they're not sitting and thinking about it. They were out there doing it.

I actually think I was realistic in not jumping out of my well-paying job into coaching again. I started contracting as I worked. I assigned myself coaching days. Because if you jump the ship, burn the bridge, your business needs time to grow. You have to be really clear about what you are doing, think smart. Wealthy successful women have multiple strings of income, so if you're still contracting AND building your business…well done. That's a really smart thing to do.

You came down with Bell's Palsy. Was that the light switch that said, OMG, my body is so overly stimulated right now! What made you flip that switch?

It was the perfectionism. I was so desperate having had two failed businesses already. The pursuit of caring what everyone thought about me. What if I failed again? So, I started pushing the perfectionism again. I was working all hours (I don't even think I was breathing properly). So, of course, my body was like, 'hey Nat, can you slow down?' and I'm like, 'Nooo, I've got to prove things.' (LAUGHS).

What I learned from Bell's Palsy was that it can be from being chronically run down. It ended up being a lot like shingles, where it attacked the nerves as opposed to coming out on my skin. It's amazing how much an illness will make you really slow down and check. The irony of the Bell's Palsy wasn't lost on me. I was the face of my business, and I was just taking off. This whole side of my face fully collapsed down, and I thought 'I'm not so perfect now.' I still have a picture of me the day after I was diagnosed looking like a drunken pirate. I was talking out of the corner of my mouth, saying let's just go. If I hadn't moved through it, I would have fallen into depression. It taught me to show up as me. If you're the expert on what you're teaching, you're going to know exactly what you need to say.

> "This whole side of my face fully collapsed down, and I thought 'I'm not so perfect now.'"
> — Nat Tolhopf

I think as female entrepreneurs, we find ourselves in that overdrive constantly. I know I have fallen victim to that several times. We just go, go, go. There is a ladder going non-stop to the ceiling and I'm going to keep climbing it. But, at some point, you have to stop. You have to slow down and take care of you, making yourself a priority.

We have so much to consume online these days from podcasts to webinars. There's so many 'shoulds' that we forget to listen to ourselves as our own leaders in our businesses. So, when we drive from other people's agendas, it's harder work. We're not in our natural flow in our way of being.

As a current leading female entrepreneur, what along your journey (besides the health scares) do you see in the challenges you may be facing?

For a while it was trying to keep up with the constant changing strategies. I could feel my perfectionism going 'you have to know how to do all these things.' It was really good for me to go no, stay in your lane. Stick to what you know. Teach sales and imperfect actions. Because for me as a high achiever, I want to do all the things. But actually, that slows us down. The biggest challenge for me is when I start to feel overwhelmed. I will very quickly go look at where the perfectionist has added complexity. As soon as you add complexity, there's too many moving parts. When we strip everything back in business, it's extremely simple. So, I'm always simplifying. I still have to check myself. That I'm not trying to be all the things for all the people. I'm naturally a people pleaser. I want to make you feel good.

What do you see next for yourself and your business? Where do you want to take your company?

That's such a good question, Callie. As high achievers, we want to keep going and moving up the bar. But is there an end point? No, there's not. I've written a second book. The last four years I've been serving the New Zealand audience. We're a small country of four million, so over the last year, I've been branching out to more international audiences. It's really bringing my style, or me and my work, to help the rest of the world and more women to normal-ize where they are at. I think everyone's ready for some reality. Everyone is sick of the 'get rich in six weeks;' we just need to hear new things. It's being a part of things like this with you, supporting you, and I'm just so honored to be a part of it. It's really bringing my message to the world, literally.

Come on over to the U.S! There's enough room for you at the table!

As entrepreneurs, we find ourselves in the ebbs and flows of being in a position that allows us to slow down, take a step back and look at what and who becomes a priority in our lives. We begin to pull back from those we place up on the ladder, who don't really need to be there, can you relate?

Yes! I think 2020 was a time where it really leveled the playing field for so many of us. We saw countries crumbling to their knees and have seen other world-wide events that make us pause in the moment and reflect.

When we look back at our careers and see what we thought were such big, pivoting moments for us, sometimes they actually weren't. Was there ever a time where somebody told you you weren't good enough? Or this path isn't meant for you, and you did whatever you could to prove them wrong? What were some examples of that if those situations happened?

Really good question. I think a lot of our fears can come from our parents. I know my parents were worried for what I was doing again. My mum in particular would see me doing things for other people and not putting myself first. In my book, I talk about how after six weeks of running the business I have now, my mum said, 'how long are you going to stick with this for?' It was a real gut punch. She showed me that when the going got tough, the old Nat ran away. It was very confronting, but it was also a beautiful gift at the same time. As much as I was in tears at the moment, it was a really good point. That helped me stick and say I'm committed to making it work this time. When I was running a private school, I was told by the owner I wasn't a great writer, so I stuck it to him!

When we finally commit to taking that next step forward and going for it full speed ahead, what values do you think are there in that underlying realization? Is it the belief in yourself or is it the commitment that you spoke of when you're looking at the person in the face saying, 'Watch me, I got this'?

I actually think, for women, we have to get out of our heads. It was a coach that brought what I call masculine energy, that I have a lot of now, telling me that factual evidence is really important. When my mum said what she did to me, I actually thought, 'I don't know if this is going to work out.' Instead, you ask, 'how can this work?' I didn't know if it was going to, so I surrounded myself with other business women and went into memberships who were asking the same questions as me and getting help. Again, as a high achiever, we like to do things for ourselves, and it is hard to ask for help. But guess what? Sometimes, you bloody don't. I had to learn that.

So true! You just don't. Put the hammer down and give it to somebody else!

You don't need to know all the things.

No. If that is someone else's genius zone, give it to them and do what you know how to do best.

I often think if you're asking people to pay you for help and you don't know how to ask for help, then the integrity loop stops. If I'm asking for people to pay me and I don't know how to pay them, then how do I really know what that's like? A lot of people know how to do a lot of things, but in theory, they don't know how to put it into action. So, the theories are no good without the testing. Theodore Roosevelt's "The Man in the Arena" speech comes to mind. If you're not in the game, then I'm not going to listen to you. How do you really know? You don't, so take your theory and watch me!

Who were some of your role models when you were looking for other business women? Things you read, people you follow online?

She's an Australian, Denise Duffield-Thomas, and the author of Get Rich, Lucky Bitch. She's really humble and down to earth. Also, Amy Porterfield. Oprah has always been such a household name. I just love the humble heroes who are actually out there doing it. It doesn't always have to be the big people out there doing stuff.

Oh, Oprah!

How amazing is she? She just keeps going. She just has the energy to keep producing. She's actually really good at repurposing her stuff.

Yes, her team is as well (LOL).

Going back to your business, take our readers through the process of being coached by you. What can someone expect from your services?

I teach on mindset versus strategy. You can Google strategy all day long. But if your sexy mindset muscle isn't as strong, the strategies will just fall over. When we start working together, there's a lot of you talking, me listening, hearing your default stories, hearing where you need clarity and stripping the complexity of your business right back. There are things I want you to start doing. We unpack any mindset stuff that may come up. Like, oh, I'm too scared to do that. Well, why are you scared? Then, we'll unpack that. Make you feel good about it and support you while you take those actions and stretch your goals. It's as simple as that. We really need to start with confidence, taking imperfect action, and knowing who you are serving and what the problem is. We must step into it! Correct me if I'm wrong, but I think women have a hard time doing this. If we don't step into it, we won't embrace the results. Bottom line, if you're my ideal client and you work with me, you will get results. If you already have a $5k business, I can help you get to $10k. We're afraid to say those things because there's been so much fear, but you must embrace the fact that you do get a result. Otherwise, you can't ask for the money.

What are you finding is the most common fear when having discussions with potential clientele?

DOUBT. Also, confusion of where to start, imposter syndrome, who am I? Those are the biggest ones. My marketing is aimed at high achievers. Are you feeling doubt or are things not working? That is deliberately what I go out searching for. I'm a very action-based coach. It's important to empower someone that they can do this without me. You'll get lovingly butt-kicked in the right direction. As your coach, I'm your mirror! You can't unsee your own beast when you're talking to someone else. You can hear it, but you can't see it.

When working with clients, what does that time span look like?

Let's go for three months. If after the first month, you're like I am done, I am out, we just part ways. Usually after the first three months, I've had clients stay anywhere from 12 months to two years. There's accountability and support for sure, but I want you to be able to know what to do. The short answer is that there are three month and six-month programs, but you can stay as long as you want.

I love asking this next question because I think it says so much. If you had three words to describe Nat, what would they be?

I'm the biggest cheerleader. Give me some pom poms. I'm also VERY honest, as in I'll tell you what you need to hear. And fun, we'll have a lot of fun and laugh a lot. That was a cool question.

As a coach we find ourselves in that serving space, but how do you take a step back, how do you recharge for you? Yes, you have a family and that's very much a part of your life, but what does Nat need to do for HER? To make sure she keeps going.

To answer in two ways: I've built my programs and offers around my strengths and having boundaries. Because it's a strength to be a people pleaser and a perfectionist, we never want to take those things away; the issue is when you don't price them properly and you don't know your boundaries. When we work together, it's priced and timed where I can have all of me without having resentment and being paid well. Does that make sense? It's hard to turn all of you off and I try not to do that, so I built the programs so I can be all of the things for you that I want to be, but there's boundaries within those. Scope the space for what you are doing and where it is held.

Daily self-care is also important. We've got this wonderful new Australian author named Dr. Libby Weaver; she wrote a book about the rushing woman syndrome. I used to be the epitome of the rushing woman. I would take my phone to the bathroom thinking it would be efficient to be responding to someone. Or driving in my car listening to podcasts. For me, I'm just learning to have some calmness every day. Journaling, mediation, breathing, looking out the window, just those little things. And of course, movement. Eating well and moving my body. It has to happen.

Are you self-sufficient with that or do you hire a trainer/nutritionist, someone to work with you so that you know you are following a plan?

I do have a trainer now because for a long time I would always go downstairs and workout but wouldn't push myself. I've learned to ask for help through fitness and I have a trainer that is amazing. There's a lot of similarities between personal trainers and business coaches; they know when to push you and they know when to say let's just do some stretching today because you seem really tired. Sometimes, we need to have those lighter days.

What are some of your guiltiest pleasures in life?

Coffee, chocolate, all the Cs…OMG that doesn't sound good. No stop, just coffee and chocolate.

That's probably one of the best answers I've had on that. (LAUGHS WITH TEARS)

What is your definition of a female entrepreneur?

Any female that is running her own business. And business doesn't have to mean you're a limited company; it could be you're a sole trader and you are out there swapping your services for money. For me, that's the simplest answer.

It takes guts.

If you have a service or product that helps others, then go and do it. It's just going to take a lot more time than you think. It doesn't happen overnight. It can take anywhere from 18 months to two years often, particularly if you are a startup. And that's okay, it's normal for it to be like that.

Final question. Finish this sentence: What if I...

Oh man. Your questions are so good, Callie, they make me think. What if I stopped being in my own way? Because we're perfectionists and we're A-types, we are constantly in our own way.

BOOM. MIC DROP.

SMOKE AND MIRRORS

Meet Melissa Moore: national best-selling author, keynote speaker, Executive Producer, and Writing Coach.

Her life's work has been Emmy-nominated. As an Executive Producer and host of Lifetime Network's *Monster in My Family*, Melissa Moore is the definition of sink or swim.

Her advocacy has captured the attention of millions across the nation through her work as a former Crime Correspondent for The Dr. Oz Show, podcast host, and the daughter of a convicted serial killer.

Her work and contributions have been shared on The Oprah Winfrey Show, Dr. Phil, Good Morning America, *People, Marie Claire,* Discovery Network and various international publications.

It is because of this woman's strength and tenacity that she has forged a new way of life, one full of meaning and purpose as she helps others heal and rise above their own compelling circumstances.

It is my pleasure to introduce you to this talented woman, mentor, and friend!

△ △ △

CK: I remember the moment our paths were connected. A Facebook post brought us together as we were in a networking group and had just missed each other at a live event in Los Angeles.

I remember reading your post and you were coaching new authors on creating book proposals! At the time I thought this was my sign! Fast forward four years later, and here we are still connected!

MM: *I'm really proud of you. I totally had forgotten that's how our paths met, as I know we also have a mutual connection.*

I find that being a part of women's masterminds is really empowering. I believe that's what got me through 2020. Being a female entrepreneur can be a lonely gig. So, getting connected with others across the industry is that much more important. Not only did it help me get through the ups and downs of business, but it also helped me answer questions when I had doubts or whether I needed to look at different strategies. When you are a part of a group, you feel supported by those who have already crossed that bridge or faced a challenge and can provide wisdom and advice. And vice versa, we also take for granted the expertise that we have and dismiss how impactful or powerful we can be to other people.

CK: Surround ourselves with those who will stand in your corner. When we have those moments and ask where am I going, who am I working with, what am I doing? I personally have found that those challenges guide me to step into something bigger. I think we can all relate to that at some point or another in our lives. For example, when you and I had our consultation. I remember pulling into a parking lot off the side of the road and knowing I was ready to do this! We were on the phone, and we clicked right away, not missing a beat. I knew I could see myself working with you in this project.

(Sidenote: Melissa helped me begin this process. I told her my vision that I had for this book. Granted, this book has transitioned in and of itself, but she helped guide me in doing market research, run comparisons, shop similar products, query agencies, etc. Because of her expertise in her own background and career, I knew she was somebody I could trust to steer me in

the right direction. When I am looking at working with a coach, I go straight to the mothership! And she was a hell yes for me!)

This book began as a planner/coaching guide. Today, it is still a coachable piece, but we also decided to feature incredible women to share their stories of true grit, stories that pull back the curtain of the facade of female entrepreneurship. Because sadly, we are marketed a different story. And this book is here to reveal that.

There is a catch phrase in this book coined 'sink or swim.' Melissa has a sink or swim story. Like some of the others featured in this book, she has also been through a traumatic life experience. I remember the day she shared her story with me, and I instantly thought this woman was a warrior, not a victim. The cards she was dealt could have gone such a different way. And, after healing and deep inner work, she has really learned how to catapult herself into another level and further her career.

If you don't mind, Melissa, will you share a synopsis of your sink or swim story?

MM: *Absolutely. In 1995, I received the devastating and shocking news that my father was arrested for serial murder. At the time, we thought it was for the murder of his fiancée, Julie Winningham. However, over the course of his trial, we discovered it was more than Julie Winningham, and there were dozens of more victims. My father assaulted many women, killed eight women that we know of, and he was known in the Pacific Northwest as the "Happy Face Serial Killer."*

I go into a lot of detail about that journey in my iHeart Media podcast, Happy Face, that came out in 2018. It was a journey that I took to meet Julie Winningham's surviving son, Don Findlay, and met with him. That took a lot of courage, but it was ultimately one of the most transformational things I did in my life. Growing up as the daughter of a serial killer, I carried a lot of shame. And of course, it caused a lot of issues for my identity. Like, who am I? You hear the saying the apple doesn't fall far from the tree, and if he's a serial killer what does that make me? What about my DNA? Over the years I have come to realize I am not what my father did, I'm not the crimes he committed, and I get to choose my own path, and one that has meaning to me.

In 2008, I decided to write my story and it was called Shattered Silence. *I took a year to write it. It was my memoir and an entire story of growing up, living with my father and his secrets and how our family came to terms with this. Then, I found myself on The Oprah Winfrey Show.*

One evening I had just finished the galley (the manuscript), and it wasn't even slated for publishing yet. That night at 10 o'clock, I was on Twitter. The executive producer for The Oprah Winfrey Show had posted a Tweet asking if anyone had any story ideas for the upcoming season? (This is a full circle moment because I now work in daytime television and know what happens behind the scenes). At the time, I wasn't working in daytime and had no knowledge of schedules and filming. For example, that part of the industry takes summers off like a teacher's schedule. And I remember Oprah was making headlines because she was doing this Mediterranean cruise and taking all of her key employees on this cruise. In the media, InTouch *and* People *magazines were covering it, and it happened to be while she was on that cruise that she read the galley from my book. Side note: I still have the Tweets that Lisa Erspamer (EP) and I exchanged, and we continued the conversation surrounding my story. Shortly after, I was booked to come on during the premier week of the season before her last on The Oprah Winfrey Show.*

CK: What was going through your head when you knew you were about to step on Oprah's stage? She was and still is one of the biggest platforms for daytime television. I can't imagine how that feels; what were you feeling at the time?

MM: *Prior to going on the show, I told my publisher for my book, 'you're not going to believe this, Oprah's going to have me on her show!' The publicist for the publishing company was like, well, that's not certain because you can get bumped out. I didn't realize that if something breaks, like a new breaking story or a major headline happens, then you can be bumped and somebody else will fill your spot. But it's unlikely because they will just record with you and move you into a new time slot or different episode.*

Even after the publicist telling me it could fall through, I just held onto the vision. This was going to happen! I remember coming home from school and turning on The Oprah Winfrey Show while having my after-school snack!

I'll never forget the quote that she's famous for which is, 'GOD can dream bigger for me, for you, than you could ever dream for yourself.' I thought this was full manifestation! I would have never dreamed I would be sitting here on her stage and talking to her. Leading up to the show, I knew I couldn't bring guests. However, I wanted to bring female empowerment. There was an amazing LGBT couple that owned a gift giving service which offered planters. The company is based in Idaho and is well-known now. At the time, I was married, and my husband told me about Potting Shed Creations, who were making these plant-based gifts. He was an executive over their shipping, so I asked if he would get a gift basket for Oprah! I brought that and added Cowgirl Chocolates to put together the gift basket. Shortly after, Potting Shed Creations ended up being chosen for Oprah's Favorite Things!

It was kind of a win-win because I had a gift to give to Oprah and they received free promotion!

You don't go to The Oprah Winfrey Show without a gift basket! LAUGHS.

She was so lovely. I remember during a commercial break, she pointed to a page and said to me that this was so well written, and this was her favorite line in my book.

I have it written in my journal what she exactly said, what that line was, but it basically pertains to what you are talking about. Which was I knew I had a choice, and the choice was either this is going to be it or I'm going to choose something else. I'm not going to follow in this generational trauma, I'm going to move past it. Those words will forever be logged in my journal, the journal that Oprah gave me.

Hearing you say this makes my eyes well up. I can't help but think about the many women who have been through similar circumstances, and who have chosen to walk away.

The front cover of this book showcases a female walking in an iconic, powerful brand: Christian Loubutin shoes. There is grit around the bottom of her feet and that is the definition of the silt that is going to try and hold you back and you get to choose.

You really do, you really do. Sometimes you just don't know how. I didn't know how I was going to be on The Oprah Winfrey Show. It manifested as I did the daily actions. There's something to be said about consistency, and I honestly believe that's 90% of my success. It's showing up every day and doing the things you need to do. That's especially true if you are wanting to write a book. You can be incredibly overwhelmed if you think of the sum of writing an entire 60,000-word book. But you won't be overwhelmed if you take it into bite size pieces every day. One thing that writing a book has taught me is that writing is rewriting. That's all it is. You write something and then you rewrite it. You take imperfect action and write whatever you want to write and come back to fix it. It is a constantly moving and fluid document. It comes to a point where you actually have to stop rewriting. You tell yourself this is good enough and you have to trust that it is, or your editor will tell you. I found that I could write an entire book if I just took small actions every day. I did that while operating a business and had two toddlers. I believe anybody can write a book and do it if they want to.

You've gone on to write more books after your first book.

Yes. My second book is called, WHOLE: A Guide to Self-Repair, *and I'm working on my third book right now with Random House. I'm writing that as I work a full-time job creating television shows. I've taken the talent that I have developed overtime of storytelling and crafted it into a way where I sell true-crime documentaries. I'll find a survivor story that's interesting to me and I will start to draft out an episodic deck of what that could look like. It is the same template as writing a book proposal. I help clients who want to share a book idea by drafting the same template for a television show as for their life in a memoir form.*

So neat. There are so many more untold stories that need to be heard.

I hear incredible stories all the time. For example, I am working with a client who witnessed her father killing her mother. Her father was sent to prison, and she was sent to the hospital because she had stab wounds from her dad trying to kill her as well. Years later, she aged out of an orphanage and became an Emmy-winning television producer. This is a woman of grit and perseverance! When I asked her about her why and the message she wanted to relay out of her book, she said to me, "save yourself. No one is coming. Save yourself."

It is so true. You really have to pick yourself; even if you are a parent, you still have to do the work to take care of yourself and not rely on some circumstances changing to make things better for you. You can change those circumstances.

> "Save yourself. No one is coming. Save yourself."
> Melissa Moore

Are you primarily working with clients who have been through traumatic experiences to share their stories?

The bulk of my clients are, however, I have some entrepreneurs that I work with that have been through severe experiences like domestic violence, and then go onto creating a multi-million dollar business. If the entrepreneurs don't have a crime aspect but have a life moment or crisis that has changed their life significantly and they want to impart that wisdom to people, I need to make sure that comes with genuine intent. As you know, writing a book is a labor of love and you have to be incredibly driven to want to share your message and help other people. In the beginning stages, it is similar to building a non-profit business.

For a long time!!

It has to be a passion project because divine timing will bring it into fruition. These projects require investment, money, and belief. When I see women step up and put investment money into their beliefs, I think that is incredibly powerful.

When we want to go to another level, we have to invest in that level. We have to invest in those mentors that are going to help us into that new level. We are paying for their expertise and time so we can get on the fast track to success. It is hard to find others who are truly legitimate with what they can offer; however, looking at my business now, I wish I would have had a mentor back then.

One of my biggest drivers behind this book is to show what really goes on behind the scenes for hard-working, female entrepreneurs who are committed to stepping up. Even as coaches, we have to give ourselves that grace knowing we have something to offer to give to others. What do you think is one of the biggest myths you've seen in the coaching world?

I think the biggest myth (or the smoke and mirrors of it) is that it's full of glamor, designer outfits, and $10K months: I see that all the time. And, if it's not easy, then you are doing something wrong. THAT is a false narrative. Being an entrepreneur is not always easy. You are going to have to break out of your comfort zone, talk to people that you don't want to talk to, or have hard conversations. You are going to have days where you doubt yourself and wonder if this is even what you are supposed to be doing, why you may be messing up, or why can't it be easy like it is for that coach? However, there is a component where I think it should be fun. Talking to you is fun, working with my clients is fun, so I don't feel the labor of showing up to a job I despise, yet it doesn't go without some hurdles.

Can you recall a moment or a time where you started to doubt yourself?

Sooo many times, let me pick one! LAUGHS.

There are so many to choose from!

Not everything I have accomplished has been tremendously successful. My first podcast with iHeart Media, Happy Face, hit 22 million downloads! Then, I wanted to branch out and do something on my own terms, so I left and created another podcast, Life After Happy Face. Dr. Laura Pettler, a Forensic Criminologist, and I began connecting with everyday people that had a true crime story or were able to talk about their lives with a killer or having been a victim. In the beginning, Dr. Laura and I funded it ourselves with the promise that we would be reimbursed. We had a contract with a small-time media company to help fund it and then it fell through. This led to having hard conversations about leaving, receiving a severance, and following through on our contracts.

That was one of my biggest learning lessons! I don't regret that investment. It showed me that I don't have to wait on somebody else (like a media company) to get the job done. However, I did doubt myself afterwards. I thought that this podcast was a one hit wonder; maybe that is as good as it gets and even if podcasting was something I would do again.

Then I heard the quote, 'your best work is never behind you.' If you're breathing, your best work is still yet to come. I don't have all of the answers or how that lesson will manifest itself into a better outcome, but I know it is for the greater good. We need to keep moving forward through the challenges in search of something that is a better fit.

One of our other collaborators in this book speaks on how we never have failed if something doesn't pan out. Just because we leave something doesn't mean you have failed. It just taught you more lessons of what you didn't want or need in your life at that time. I whole-heartedly believe that. Having heard your journey and those challenges, what are the next steps for you? Where do you see yourself producing and creating even bigger work in front of you?

This is going to be my best year yet! I've already sold two documentaries and one movie! The level of stories that we are sharing have exceeded anything else I have ever done. Currently, I am working with two female clients, one that has a 16-hour documentary and movie coming out on Lifetime in 2023. We are in negotiations right now for the other client and Lifetime, as hers has a bidding war for what network it will go to. Because of non-disclosures I can't share all the details I would love to share, so I'm trying to be elusive.

Yes, don't get yourself in trouble! LAUGHS.

In these contracts there are NDAs and you can't reveal anything. The project becomes confidential, so it doesn't get injured by another company trying to make a spin-off of it or copy.

As the conduit in helping your clients share their messages on a television platform, what does your role entail?

I am the executive producer. This is similar in how we worked together. When someone approaches me with a story and I know that story needs to be heard in the form of a documentary, I will then craft it and write it in the form of a TV deck. To assist me in the process, I have partnered with a big production company so that I don't have to keep overhead on camera gear or staff. Once I pitch them my idea, we are able to use their funds and my contracts to merge into an intellectual property in order to create a sizzle reel. A sizzle reel is similar to a movie trailer for the story. The production company I have worked with for these projects is Marwar Junction Productions. They are based out of Los Angeles, California and have an amazing, talented group of executives that came from daytime television's Rachael Ray show. I am working on one of my client's shows with them. Since we have pitched the concept, the project has now become a documentary and a movie and we have since sold it! Since we are both the executive producers, I then get to make the decision if I want to stay on and work on the project, or if somebody else takes the reins and brings the work to fruition. Lately, I have been making the choice to forgo working on these projects, so I am able to bring forth other stories and work with more women.

At some point, you do have to look at what's in front of you and weigh the work of what takes more precedence. All our work lives and schedules are set up so differently, and I know you have an incredibly busy schedule. What does your day-to-day look like?

I wake up at 4:30 a.m. so that I have a time slot to myself for journaling, meditation, gratitude, and setting my intentions for the day. For me it's non-negotiable, I have to do it. It's my self-care. I get grumpy if I don't get it in! I do it first thing in the morning so something else doesn't take its place. Since I get up so early, I also go to bed at 8 or 8:30 p.m.

We do that at our house all the time!!!

My kids make fun of me. They'll say, 'it's eight o'clock, you're so old, Mom.' Well, I get up at 4:30 so I'm tired. LAUGHS.

My daughter is in her early 20s, so she works and is self-sufficient. My son goes to high school, so once I get him off to school, I work out. That is another non-negotiable. Afterwards, I go straight into emails and Zoom calls until two p.m. Between my calls, I'll often do follow-up work. This could be pitching a show to a network executive or working with a DNA specialist on a cold case. I also record potential stories to pitch, so then I have to transcribe and write it to work it into a deck. Once my family comes home, I make dinner, and then recharge by having a glass of wine while watching 90-Day Fiancé or Real Housewives!

I also recharge by watching Real Housewives! I DVR them on purpose!

I've noticed the Real Housewives are constantly drinking wine, so maybe that's why I have my glass as I watch them! LAUGHS.

It's subliminal messaging to all of us who get sucked into their lives!

Last time you and I chatted, you were working on The Dr. Oz Show...

Yes, The Dr. Oz show has come to an end. He is going into politics so that chapter has ended. I'm no longer the Crime Correspondent for the show. This is a new direction where all of my time is spent working on documentaries being an executive producer. I'm loving it!

All of your work has come full circle! Everything you've dived into, whether you were the correspondent, writing books, coaching others, pitching stories... At the end of the day, if you had to step back and look at your life and how you are serving, how does that make you feel? What do you see?

I am so happy every day, I can't even tell you. It's so remarkable to me that I get to have a job where I work with people who have survived incredible circumstances, who are choosing to make different lives for themselves or use that horrific event to help others. There is nothing more rewarding than this. I love this industry; I truly think I have the best job in the world! I don't have to commute on the freeway to sit at a desk, and nobody tells me what to do. Granted, when I am immersed in a story, I tend to go down the rabbit hole as I read all the books and watch the videos! I get really engrossed in a story I am producing or want to work on! If I am working with a client on their story, there can be a lot of hand holding in the form of coaching and guidance. It is scary for people when they are first coming out with their story. I remember how terrified I was of public judgment; I didn't want people thinking I was this horrible person. You hope by coming forward it doesn't change your story in a negative way. So, I absolutely understand my clients' fears, they are not irrational.

I don't think people think about the emotional aspect in coming forward. Unfortunately, society has shown us differently in a variety of circumstances. Personally, I'll connect with somebody because of who they are and not outside

circumstances, so when I hear that from you, it makes me emotional knowing we can do better. That way of pre-judgment has to go.

Exactly. For example, the media will already have a narrative about a family in a high-profile case. Let's take the Laundries and the Gabby Petito case. The media spun their own narrative about Brian Laundrie's parents. Now, there is a storyline in regard to what they knew and what they didn't know. In the moment, they had never stepped forward to tell their side of the story. I don't have judgment for that; however, the media will fill in those blanks, so it leads people to converse. It is a game of clickbait. What propels me to keep going is to know the truth within the story. This is a classic example if his parents were a client of mine. I would have to find out what the truth is and compare the differences between their real experience and what was perceived, so that we could share the story in a way that people care.

Is there a project that you have not been a part of that you would really like to work on?

I have been corresponding with Susan Smith for years. She was convicted of murdering her two sons by drowning them in a South Carolina Lake. [As of this 2022 interview, Susan Smith has never spoken out and is eligible for parole as early as 2024.] Her story is incredibly fascinating to me. After her father committed suicide, her stepfather sexually abused her until she was in her 20s. When she went to trial for her conviction, he came forward and confessed to what was coined incest. I believe it wasn't incest, it was sexual abuse. He assaulted her. We have seen cases where terminology greatly dismisses acts of trauma.

Smith was also exploited in prison by a guard who was having sexual contact with her. It was becoming an abuse of power. The prison doctor and the warden discovered she had an STD, and that prison guard was removed from his job. Because of this scandal, it also revealed that this was problematic in other prisons, as guards were having sex with inmates away from the property while working public service projects.

Sadly, I believe that is happening in more places than we even want to admit or look into.

From a true crime space and story perspective, I have to look at how she became this woman who killed her children. The public may look at her and think she is a horrible monster. I'm not making excuses as to why she did it, I just have to understand what causes a mother to want to kill her sons.

You have to understand the psychological connection.

I allow my curiosity to guide me to the stories I want to work on. Sometimes it leads me to a victim/survivor or a perpetrator.

You definitely have a gift for working in this niche. There are not a lot of people who wake up one day and say this is what I want to do with my life.

I didn't know that I would be immersed in this world. In 2008, I was afraid of people knowing about this horrible thing that had happened to my family and me. I had no idea it would lead me to living this amazing, fulfilling career of working with people and helping them share their stories.

Fortunately for yourself and your clients, you all have a medium to share your side of the story. Knowing what you know now, what would be your message to others who fear being judged who have also been through similar life events?

Honestly, be who you are. At the end of the day, this is the experience you get to live, and you can make it what you want it to be. I think there is so much fear in how we will be perceived either by the people we love and admire, or others in general. I used to live in fear. I thought that if I came forward, people are going to think I am a horrible person or I wanted fame. But they didn't know what my intentions were. If I would have let that stop me, I wouldn't be where I am today.

To come forward is a hard place to sit in. You have to do it in a way that feels right for you and follow that intuition. Be yourself and accept that we are all flawed human beings. It is okay, I know my flaws and am aware of how to work with them.

Don't we all? LAUGHS. Just tuck them in your back pocket:)

As a writing coach, you have been able to take authors around the world on writing retreats. I know Italy and Morocco have made the list!

Yes! I had this vision and dream of going to Morocco for years. Finally, I made it happen last year by going to scout the location for this last retreat.

When I told people I wanted to go to Morocco, the responses weren't very supportive. I was told how dangerous it was for a female! Sadly, I started to believe it; however, I still wanted to go! I went last summer and had an amazing time. Morocco was unlike anything I have ever experienced, and I have gone all over the world! I've traveled to Capri, Italy, Bali, and other many beautiful places. Morocco was from another world; it was like going back to medieval times. Many items are still made by hand.

The day we arrived, "Eid Al-Adha" was being celebrated. In the Muslim calendar, this is one of the most important and greatest festivals. It is a festival of sacrifice where Muslim families that can afford it sacrifice a sheep.

In hindsight, my American culture was shocked! It was one of the most barbaric things I have ever seen. We arrived on a giant slaughter day! The streets are filled with celebration and people are prepping by sharpening knives with a rock on a wheel. They bring a sheep to slaughter and give portions of it to those less fortunate. Every single part of the animal is saved and eaten. All of the perishable parts are placed in a bag and given to homes. The other bits are hung outside to dry for days in the sun to be used later. That day it was nearing a 100 degrees, so there was a distinct smell…

Like Kansas City BBQ! (Kidding).

Another level! During our stay, we also went through the Souks and one of the medinas. We rode camels in the desert! The people are beautiful and kind. I felt safe.

Like most places, you learn about the street culture and schemers. I learned very quickly that you can't look lost. Someone will try to guide you to the place you want to see, and once they take you there, they want money. If you don't pay them money, they get very upset. Because the Souks feels like a giant maze without street names, it is very easy to look and get confused. You learn to not allow anyone to guide you!

During our retreat, I worked with legitimate guides, so that did not happen!

Overall, this type of environments evoke creativity, and I am so elated to have had these experiences with other women! We stayed in a traditional Riad, in the heart of Marrakesh.

You are providing service in so many ways, I can't thank you enough for sharing this time between you and me to dive deeper. Melissa, you are the definition of sink or swim.

Thank you.

Knowing where my own vision got started, I could not have thought of yet another amazing female to feature in this piece. Thank you from the bottom of my heart.

Thank you for giving me this opportunity; it's always lovely to see you and I couldn't be more proud of what you are doing!

BREAKING THE BARRIER

Meet Jodie Rodenbaugh: Life Liberator, Master of Emotional Intellect, and one hell of a game changer!

When I asked Jodie to be a part of this piece, I believe the first words out of my mouth were, "the world needs to hear you." Not only have I been a personal client, but I have also witnessed her surrealistic talent in working with women who have been held back from decades of childhood and emotional trauma. Today, those women stand in their purpose, giving themselves permission to lead lives with a new set of standards.

Rodenbaugh's story is one of hope, breaking barriers, and the truths we all need to hear. Take notes, ladies!

△   △   △

JR: *I decided at a very young age I was going to do life and love different. I was a rebel in a sense. It wasn't that I was doing anything wrong, I just wasn't doing it your way.*

When we survive childhood trauma, we don't think of it as trauma. My mother stepped away from her own personal power when I was a child; she gave up on herself. Watching this at such a young age, I decided I was going to be loved and allow myself to be loved even though that was not my experience. It is the emotional self-regulation that my parents didn't have. It's not that my parents were humble people, it's because they didn't know what they didn't know. This also served as a turning point for me to not use this as an excuse and why I would allow unconditional love into my adult life.

CK: Do you feel that as a society we tend to hold onto these types of excuses, which ultimately can and will hold us back from moving forward in our lives?

JR: What I do best is to help people go back and find the core cause of why they are feeling stuck and can't move forward, why they feel like they keep hitting their heads on a brick wall.

CK: At one point or another in our lives, we all have felt 'stuck.' Tell us about a moment or chapter in your life where you have felt stuck.

JR: It was during the marriage of my first story, my first husband. I was married to an amazing man and father of two children at the time. I was at a point where I felt stuck in our love. I wanted to be an amazing wife and run into his arms, full of pure joy and love. But I couldn't. I was afraid to love. To be vulnerable in love, it made no logical sense.

At the time, I was a pioneer of emotional intelligence. I was a teacher, teaching children to be emotionally intelligent. However, I was unable to apply this at home. It wasn't a therapy issue; I didn't want to sit in the thing. I saw it as something I was entangled in. Once I finally saw the core cause and could pick out the pieces from my history, that's when the work began, and I started to feel confident in the kind of love I was able to not only receive but also give.

What happened next?

Once I had cracked the code, it wasn't until I was 15 weeks pregnant with our third child, that my husband had gone in for a routine rotator cuff surgery. While waiting for him, I found out he was accidentally injected with the anesthesia into his main artery. He died that day.

When my husband died, I left my body. I was looking down at myself (like we see in the movies) and my soul was dying. Here I was holding my pregnant belly for truly the first time. That's when I really learned what unconditional love really was. I fell in love with myself for the first time. It was my father-in-law's voice that screamed out, 'My grand babies!' and that is what brought me back into my body.

Here you were raising two children under the age of five and about to deliver your third six months later. How did you begin to cope?

I learned how to do self-hypnosis for delivery. Anesthesia was not an option! I went through 19 hours of zero pain! It wasn't until the last 30 minutes of my delivery when I lost my mind and emotions. I realized what pain actually was in the mind. It is what we create in our minds; I was out of control of my body. The experience of this delivery taught me how to grieve and how life and death fit all together. When death happened, I literally had life inside of me. As women, we get to hold life, we hold the universe inside.

So true. We can forget as women what capable and miraculous human beings we are. Here you are holding this new gift of life while also grieving in the process. Looking back, what did this moment also teach you?

After my husband died, I made him three promises that were energetic standards I wanted to believe in. They were going to place me in a growth trajectory and mindset as opposed to a fixed mindset. The bottom line: I refused for my children to become a sad statistic raised in a fatherless childhood, which could be a lot of pressure. If I have emotional mastery, anything is possible. From THAT place, I can trust myself. I can trust a partnership in life and all things. We separate from life, and we are the walking dead.

What were the energetic standards you gave YOURSELF?

1. I'm here to live. If momma is drowning, she can't save her babies from drowning either. If it's not in alignment with where I was going, it has to go!

> DECISION OVERLOAD IS WHAT I HAVE FOUND TO BE
> THAT BURNS OUT WOMEN THE MOST!

2. I'm here to love. Not on my watch was I going to be someone that would block love again. When we block, we're not allowing for it to come in and through.

3. I'm here to lead. Mother ducks lead their ducklings. How I lead them into a greater life experience no matter what has occurred in our lives.

Having set these new standards for yourself during this time, how did you find your life changing after the fact?

Two months after, I went back to my job as a STEM teacher. I was writing questions, teaching children how to ask better questions about life. I saw an image standing on one side of the bridge. It was me at a crossroads. I knew what was on the other side, I just had to walk through the fog. To go into the space of uncharted territory. The moment I knew I had outgrown the brick box I was in (public school education), was like sitting down putting pieces of a puzzle together. After completion, I was staring back at an image of myself!

I REALIZED THE ANSWERS ARE NOT IN THE BOOKS, NOT IN THE SCHOOLS. THEY ARE ALREADY HERE.

We just have to know how to untangle what is blocking us from our true genius. So, I left.

Where does this leave you today?

I am in a place in this lifetime to stand in my whole, complete purpose. I am here to liberate people, the life and love that they come to experience, and that includes me. Sometimes we have to go under to get over. I am also married to my second story. My husband now and I are creating legacies in our businesses, where no one in our families' histories have ever been in a place to do so. I play in the realms of possibilities and potentialities. What is predictable is no longer for me.

Do you believe you play in these realms because you've given yourself permission to do so?

Absolutely, 100%. When we realize we don't need the protective armor and mechanisms, we are who we are because we're worthy. We deserve because we deserve; we are made of life and potentiality. When we put ourselves upon the shelf, we are separating from the source.

Why are we placing ourselves on the shelf? Is it the stigma our society and cultures have placed upon us? Or do we just get stuck there emotionally? Does it really come down to just choosing whether to be on the shelf or not to be on the shelf?

Yes, all of it. We are breaking old paradigms in this place in history. We cannot use old masculine tools anymore. For example, I tell money what to do, not Big Daddy. I am creating it. We put ourselves on the shelf when we don't feel as though we are enough.

We are personally responsible for where we belong. It's not what someone has done to us. It's what we have decided to tell ourselves about that. The feeling, we either accept or reject. We hand over our power to other people.

If you don't belong on the shelf, get off the shelf! If you don't understand the energetic standard of where you belong, you will never get there.

I gave myself no other options but my energetic standards. The decision to get where you are going, who you are to get there, combined with the feeling is why we're here. When you have to cross that bridge, it's not going to feel good. You're changing the cellular memory in your body.

The next level is not going to look the same. Most of us make decisions on what we're used to versus what we are not!

The wisdom comes from when you cross over the bridge. If you get what you expect, you really didn't cross the bridge; the expectation is a predictable path.

How do we get across?

The HOW is not our business yet. Until we know the first step and have gone where no one in your ancestral lineage has gone, your body is going to fight, flight, or freeze. People will stop here because they do not feel ready. Something of a lower nature has to die in order for that next step to happen. You're going to wonder how you did it until you're standing in it, wondering how you did it.

> "If you get what you expect, you really didn't cross the bridge; the expectation is a predictable path."
>
> Jodie Rodenbaugh

You decide I am the kind of woman who _____. You are the author of your life, the authority.

If we want to experience heaven on earth, we cross the bridge!

You're going to do it. Because that's the kind of woman you are. If you feel like your purse is caught in the elevator downstairs…

You packed a little too heavy and have some work to do!

If you tap into the truths, your heart of hearts, and your soul of souls, it is the scary AF yeses you get to experience! You know it is a yes to the other side.

Are you going to sit back and read your story with grateful tears in your eyes saying, 'well played?'

Your legacy is how you choose to live today. You get to write this story, your story. You set the standard for your own life and inspire others to follow along the way.

It is scary as hell to go first. But you know it right away because you know who you are.

SevenDays

MAKE A RIPPLE, CHANGE THE WORLD

DRIVE

Meet Mindy Corporon: Co-Founder and President of SevenDays® Inc., a 501c3, author, and Co-Founder of Workplace Healing LLC.

Mindy Corporon is the definition of sink or swim. She has experienced the emotional, raw pain of losing both her father and son in a way most of us cannot fathom. It was nearly a decade ago that Corporon's family was greatly affected by one of Kansas City's most eminent hate crimes.

What hasn't been taken from her is her willingness and God-gifted power to continue in helping others heal through their own grief-filled journeys.

Over the years, Corporon has relayed her story of soul-searching survival across the nation. Today, as she shares her story with you, it is my hope that we all do better and be kinder to one another.

Author of *Healing a Shattered Soul,* I introduce Mindy Corporon.

△   △   △

CK: *Come Sweat or Silt* goes beyond the basics of a book title. It is about the journey we all take, and the sweat equity we have put into the years behind us. The silt is the stuff that tries to stop you along the way, that gathers beneath your feet. Through the dirt and the grind, you are the one who gets to decide how you will move past the silt. Sharing all your stories and how you landed where you are today is the tribute in these pages. It makes me think back to

the very beginning when we were little and were asked what we wanted to be when we grew up. What was your dream for you as a child?

MC: *I wanted to be an astronaut! I majored in aeronautical engineering. When I graduated high school, I wanted to be an astronaut. Except my eyesight was very bad. I could have been considered legally blind and had worn corrective eyewear from the time I was ten. My parents at the time didn't realize I could not see until we were playing a car game, one of those driving games. For example, can you spot such and such on a sign. I think I said, "What sign?" When they asked me again, I was like I'm not seeing what you are seeing. After they tested me, they realized I could hardly see in front of me. Everything was blurry. I bring this up because I also thought I wanted to go into the Air Force. However, that wasn't going to happen either because I get a little air sick and I'd be vomiting all the time. So, that's when I searched on how to be an astronaut. Prior to being in my teens, I also wanted to ride in the rodeo. I loved horses. I barrel-raced when I was nine and was certain I would be a cowgirl of some kind on a ranch.*

CK: You and I share a similar past time. I also barrel-raced here and there when I was younger. During that time, a good friend of mine and her family owned a ranch. They were really big in the sport.

Did you realize you couldn't see while you were in school?

MC: *I was in fifth grade at the time. I guess what I had done was self-acclimated, and I had always put myself in the front of the class. When my teachers would start writing on the chalkboard and I couldn't see it, I guess they just said come closer. No one ever reported that I couldn't see and I always sat in the front of the class. In fact, all the way into my adult years working at Boynton Corporon Wealth Management, which is now known as BCWM, anytime we go to any conference, everyone knows I sit in the front row. I always sit up front, ready to engage and ask questions. I think it was a habit because when I was in elementary school and I couldn't see, I had to sit in the front row. When I first got my glasses, I walked outside, looked at a tree and could see the leaves! I had not known what a tree truly looked like. I didn't know there were individual leaves. I just thought it was a glob of green whooshing around.*

Here I was tiny me, with this boy cut short hair looking like John Denver discovering what a tree looked like!

Too good! I can just picture that!

You mentioned that you were in wealth management for quite some time. How long were you in the corporate sense of working?

I graduated in December of 1990 from college. In 1991, I became employed in Kansas City. I had several different jobs. I worked in economic development, and soon after I was employed at a brokerage firm; they were a penny stock firm called Berthel Fisher & Company. I worked for them, then moved to Kidder, Peabody & Co., to PaineWebber and then to H&R Block Financial Advisors. Finally, from H&R Block Financial Advisors to Boynton Corporon Wealth Management. I left the corporate world in 2018 and really ramped up Mindy Corporon, LLC. I started working full-time on SevenDays® Inc, the 501c3, previously known as Faith Always Wins Foundation. Although it had been going since 2014, I had been working on it part-time. You see, I was working full-time on our foundation as I was creating my personal brand, Mindy Corporon LLC. Hired as a keynote speaker for events, it was clear that many people wanted to hear my story about the murders of Dad and Reat. In 2020, I authored Healing a Shattered Soul, allowing the devastation that these murders caused our family to be documented for all to read. Making my way back to corporate America was a quicker transition than I had expected. An idea I had in 2017 led to the opening of Workplace Healing LLC, a B2B SaaS company in 2018.

When you first began Mindy Corporon, LLC., did you ever envision yourself becoming an entrepreneur? Was that even in your line of work for you?

Yes. I had already been an entrepreneur in the corporate world. My business partner and I, Richard Boyer, at Kidder, Peabody & Co, he, and I partnered and left, going to PaineWebber. When you are an investment advisor in the wealth management space, you're very entrepreneurial. You have to create your own brand. You can trade through a broker dealer, such as Charles Schwab or Bank of America. While you rely on the broker dealer for many operations, you are encouraged and expected to brand yourself because we were a Registered Investment Advisor. Boyer Corporon Wealth Management is its own entity.

I was an entrepreneur even in elementary school! I created a newsletter for our street. I thought it was important that everyone on our street knew what was going on. So, I had a notepad and would go house-to-house, jotting down what was going on in people's lives. Then I would go rewrite all of it and make copies at my dad's office to hand them out. I was eight at the time!

I think they call that the neighborhood gossip!

That's what I was doing. I was spreading the news! Then, when I was in college, I opened a company. It was called Cheer Stuff.

Side note: my brain is always thinking about how something could work better. How something could be better and more efficient. Even if I'm walking on the beach and I see there's a lot of trash, I will begin thinking of a way to have it cleaned effectively. For instance, if every beach walker were handed a small trash sack for their walk and asked to pick up 6-20 items each, consider how much trash would find its way to a receptacle on the way out of the beach. I think of things like this all the time.

Going back to my college business! I had been a high school cheerleader in a really small town in Oklahoma. Marlow, Oklahoma. When you go to cheerleading camp, you had to dress alike every day. Shorts, t-shirts, hair bows, socks, to the color of ten-nis shoes. We all had to look exactly alike. In Marlow, our only shopping space was Wal-Mart. We didn't have easy access to Dallas or Oklahoma City. So, we all had to drive quite a ways to get our clothing apparel to look alike.

When I was in college, I was a cheerleader and taught cheerleading camps. There were a lot of young girls coming from rural town like I did, and they were struggling to find the apparel they wanted. So, I created an apparel company that was very specific to helping rural cheerleaders get the outfits they needed. I created stencils for what they wanted on the shirts; I bought the t-shirts and shorts in different colors and stenciled them. I would even brand them, put their name on, and sold them. I sold them around the state of Oklahoma and did that for probably 18 months. It was a growing business. I was overseeing it by myself, all the while finishing college.

I was entrepreneurial very early on in my life. I had a lot of good lessons from that job, in particular, that I'll share. One valuable lesson was when I did not get an order in. I had ordered it correctly, but the shorts were not the right shorts for this one squad. So, when I delivered the order, I delivered the right shirts and the wrong shorts. The sponsor wasn't there for me to tell her what had happened. At the time, I wrote a note, left it, and the next Monday I got a phone call. She was HOT! I didn't blame her and took the heat. I don't remember what I wrote in the note, but I'm guessing I didn't take all the blame. I didn't give her any blame, but I also didn't take ownership of giving them the wrong thing. I just learned about communicating better when we make a mistake and being forthright about any mistakes I make. Almost to a fault now if I make a mistake, I am so quick to say, 'I made a mistake, this is what I did.' Most of the time, people are like okay, it's alright. But I learned that in such a fierce way as a 20-year-old with an adult sponsor who had been a good client, and that experience had not gone well. Looking back, I don't remember everything she said, but I do remember the feeling I had, and it was so painfully embarrassing to be talked to in that way and realize that I had messed up so big.

The other thing I learned was that people cheat. People will lie and steal. I didn't know this at the time, of course. I had yet to experience it. I had this folder full of all my designs and I went to a school to have a meeting and showed them the folder of designs. Some of the cheerleaders were not at our meeting. Their sponsor asked if she could photocopy the designs for the others to see them. I gave them the book, they copied the designs, and brought me the book back. Two days later when I called them, they told me they were not going to order after all. When I showed up for a camp that their school was hosting, they were wearing my designs and clothing. I was appalled. I had no idea that an adult sponsor would teach her cheerleaders that that was okay. So, I called my parents, explained what had happened, and my dad mentioned that we know Judge Jerry Askins, why don't you call her? She was at the Stevens County Courthouse. I had interned for her one summer when I was in high school. I called her and she wrote a letter for me on her letterhead. The girls weren't able to wear the apparel with my designs on them any longer. I didn't get anything back for it, but I felt good that I confronted the problem. I felt so badly for the cheerleaders who had been taught that lesson.

Even those lessons have been valuable in helping set your foundation and business later in life. Sadly, you have to have protection. There are so many cookie cutters out there, especially in the online world. A lot of us are trying to sell the same services, just with a different face. You do have to be careful.

It becomes about relationships. In your statement about how many of us are trying to resolve the same thing but we have a different face, that's why it's so important to have a good working relationship with people who want to pay you for your value. For example, why would someone want to pay me for speaking? I need to be valuable. I need to offer that and inspiration. Most recently, I had a speaking engagement in Tampa, Florida. I asked them each time they were having me speak, who is the audience and what message do I have that is important that you think I should be delivering? Callie, I told my story six times in three days. Every time I told it, I told it with a different lens. When I spoke to the teenagers, I spoke about the importance of mental health because my younger son was 12 when my dad and Reat were murdered. We had a huge mental health crisis in our family. He was suicidal at 13 and 14 years old.

At the event, there were three sets of teenagers that I spoke to, seventh and eighth graders, ninth graders, and a teen youth group. All of them got the story, but the lens was around mental health, caring for themselves, and finding their voice to explain to other people who they are and then to listen with curiosity about who other people are. There were also other groups I spoke to; young adults, leaders, and they each got a little bit of a different lens of what I've learned in the last nine years from the murders. My point is that they could have hired any speaker. I know when I get hired, I want to offer value when someone pays for my time. I want them to remember the feeling that I leave with them even though they may not remember what I say. For me, that is always to help them be better in some way, to inspire them and understand that we all have a path to healing, and we just have to keep seeking it. It's okay to pivot, it's okay to adapt, but to always keep seeking it. Those are things that I try to convey, and I just do it in several ways.

Do you often talk to younger adults and youth ages about this? Or is this a newer run for you in speaking with a younger audience?

The youngest group I have spoken to are 13-year-olds. However, this time there were 12-year-olds. I speak to whoever hires me. I was a speaker and resident for the whole weekend in Tampa. I was with a Jewish congregation, and it was a sisterhood who had hired me to be there. Since I was going to be there for a couple of different key things, they added their youth group and young adults. With the teens, I focused a lot on them finding their voice and understanding mental health.

I think that is so incredible because there is so much of that going on around us. So much is unspoken, and sadly we have seen that rise in that younger age group. For you to really want to convey that and to hopefully leave them with that feeling of being more open and getting to know somebody, I just think that's so important in today's youth. As a community we are growing that message, and I don't think there could ever be enough.

Thank you.

You mentioned we are all on different paths to healing. When you think back to those moments to where you all were in that time of your life and where you are now, what do you think has been the biggest factor in helping you and your family heal through a life-altering tragedy?

The most important thing for me has been my belief in heaven, that dad and Reat are in heaven and that I'll see them again. I just know with all of my being that I will see them physically again and that I'll be able to hug them again and, in the meantime, there's a new energy. I had faith originally, I knew that I would see them again. I remember standing at my mailbox, (it must have been the third week after) I was crying all the time; tears were literally pouring out of me all the time. My neighbor walked over and wanted to hug me. I said, 'thank you, I know I'm going to see them, it's just going to be a really, really long time. He was just 14 and it's going to be a long time.' She said, 'It's so amazing you know you're going to see them.' I don't know that I would feel and know it, like you do.'. (She's also a Christian) "I replied with, 'I do, I feel it all over me, they are still with me.'"

I have to say the number one thing that helped me survive is that! And, at the same time, there's an energy new to me that I didn't understand before, I never explored it, and they give me messages all the time. I see yellow butterflies and deer, hear songs and things that people say or perhaps that they might wear…each of these offer me meaningful messages. Even when I was in Tampa, I was at dinner with the two women who were my hostesses. We were chatting about the foundation and different things, and all of a sudden, one of the first songs Reat ever sang live came on the radio. It's 'Drive,' by Train. It came on and I said, 'Stop, this is Reat's song!' They were like, what do you mean?

When I am places and there is music playing, one of his songs will come on. There are only three main songs that he sang. Two of them were Bruno Mars and then the song by Train.

Fast forward to the next morning and I told them about messages and how important numerology was. Numbers that are important to me are 4 and 13. They were murdered on April 13th. For example, 04 and 13 or 413, and then Reat's birthday, 5-21. My dad's birthday is January 10th. The numbers 5, 21, 4 and 13 come up all the time.

The next morning, the kids in the seventh and eighth grade group came to sit down. There was a girl who walked in with a jersey on, and it had a 13 on it. It's a Buccaneers jersey with the number 13, so it's not Tom Brady! I said, 'Look, she's wearing 13!'

The next morning, one of my hostesses (who swims every morning) had EarPods for underwater. Sometimes they gave her trouble, like a Pandora mix, and it would play and sometimes it wouldn't. When she swam that day, she told me the Train song came on. She said, 'I don't ever hear that song and I've heard it twice in the last two days.' She heard it on her Pandora mix while she was swimming!

The fact that I knew immediately that they were in heaven…I knew they were safe, cared for and loved. I knew they were not sad. When I am alone and feel that energy and receive those messages, it is so overarching.

The women and men who came into our lives and took care of us at that time were monumental. They helped breathe life back into our family and I couldn't have done it without them. It was that short time period where they lift you up and they help you walk again, help you get dressed again, help you eat again, and then once you're on your own, what do you grab onto?

I hear very similar stories from people that are deeply connected with their family and loved ones who have crossed to the other side. A good friend of mine, her first husband passed, and he comes back in the message of a fly. The fly will be sitting on the tip of a finger. You say you hear his voice in the Train and Bruno Mars songs…one of my friends just recently lost her dad tragically and she posted the other day about hearing a song. I full heartedly believe that those are messages from up above. It's how we stay connected. Even though our loved ones are no longer here on this physical planet with us, that relationship never ends. It never does.

Right. I believe that fully, that's why I walk forward every day. Because I know I'm doing what I'm supposed to be doing. I do listen to my heart a lot. I'll write things down and say to myself, 'how do I feel about that?', 'how do I feel if I do this?" How do I feel if I don't do it? I trust myself much more than I probably trusted myself eight years ago. Because I've managed to survive so much, I'm pretty kick ass.

When I feel those feelings, I know what to do with them. Does that mean I don't cry? Absolutely not. But I do know based on what I've survived so far, I can survive anything.

Without a doubt.

I had the pleasure of seeing you at a speaking engagement and getting to know your story more at your book signing. Tell our readers about your book. When did you feel the nudge to share your story and really put that into print? What made you do that?

It's interesting. Maybe four weeks after the murders, a couple of friends of mine said, 'you need to write a book about this. Your faith and inspiration are so deep, you're going to write a book.' I was exhausted at the time and barely walking, breathing, and eating. They planted that in my head that I had a story to tell. I had started journaling two days after they were murdered. I have six journals that are full. I noticed that writing out my feelings helped me.

In 2016, I wrote and wrote and wrote. I thought I was writing a book. I had help from another woman, and she and I turned it into an agent. The agent said it was a horrible story, I'm so sorry about this tragedy, you're a good writer, but it doesn't have a story arc. It's not going to keep anyone engaged. They are going to read the first chapter and go oh my gosh, I can't read the rest.

So, I set it down. I didn't know if I was going to do anything else with it until the pandemic hit. When COVID shut down everyone in March, we ramped up with Faith Always Wins and our SevenDays® event. Our event had to pivot from in-person to digital in twenty days. We had to change our entire programming. I was up several nights in a row to get everything up and going, get people engaged, and teach people about Zoom. I spent time teaching one person at a time how to get on a Zoom call so they could watch our program.

We did not shut down. We took off like lions chasing an animal, running so fast. April 2020 came to a close with the event and I gave myself permission to rest. The world was still at a somewhat pause, and I thought now's a good time, maybe I'll pick up that book and finish it. I rewrote everything, and I saw the problem. I began creating the framework. I wanted so many things to be chapters. I only thought there would be 13, but there was so much more! I wrote it to completion from July 2020 to Janu-ary 2021. I found my publisher in October 2020 via my podcast!

Because someone introduced me to someone else that did a podcast, I became a podcast host and began to interview people! As I was doing interviews, I realized I had chapters for the book. I interviewed my mom and my two brothers as those were really key to the event. Then, I interviewed my other son, Lukas, and he became two chapters.

When you have experiences and learn from them, even the challenges, you make changes.

Finding a publisher was difficult, even putting everything together to showcase the work I had done.

Tell me about it. LOL.

So many potential agents or publishers responded very quickly with a 'no, your memoir isn't in our genre. I can relate. Beginner authors can feel that across the board. It's a battlefield out there.

It's not an easy feat.

No. We received eight denials. So, I set it down. I didn't want to chase bad energy. I did a podcast with Bill Tammeus. Bill had just written another book and he had a new publisher. His publisher had heard our interview, messaged me on LinkedIn, and wanted to hear about our story. Front Edge Publishing published my book!

Initially, we had a meeting and David Crumm, Founding Editor of Front Edge Publishing (FEP) asked me to consider FEP as my publisher.

At the time, I was already done thinking about it. After three weeks, I said yes, they said yes, and we set the deadlines. I had more all-nighters getting all the photos together, editing the chapters, and making everything just as perfect as possible for printing.

How did you feel when you were done writing and you knew this was going to be delivered to the world?

TIRED. I was both mentally and emotionally exhausted. It took so much out of me to continue retelling it. My mom retold the story, my brothers Tony and Will, and Lukas. I was reliving it all over again.

In 2021, I published a book and opened a software company all in one year. That is a lot to do. I'm very proud of myself. I don't know that I can do all of that again in another year, but I'm glad that the book is out there. I also recorded the book over the summer and now it's available on Audible.

How was your experience in recording your own book?

My producer that produced my podcast is in Orlando. I went to Orlando three weekends in a row, recorded for 36 hours to get a 12-hour book. He asked me if I had listened to it, and I said no, I totally trust you, I don't want to listen to it. Pastor Adam Hamilton asked me, "if I read my book after I published it. 'No, I did not.'". I don't want to read it again. I've lived it and lived it and told it every day. It's not a book I can put away, it's my life.

> *"It's not a book I can put away, it's my life."*
> *Mindy Corporon*

For you and many others that have been through similar tragedies, it doesn't just go away. It's not a book you can put back on the shelf and close when you are done; it's open.

It's open every day. It's open every morning, it's open every second. Reat and Dad are always on my mind, always in my heart. I keep thinking when am I going to rest? I rest seven hours at a time. That's just what I do. I sleep seven hours nearly every night and that's the rest that I get.

You've been able to help yourself heal through many varietals, producing the book and more. What would you tell others that have been through similar situations? What would you want to leave them with?

I talk about that in the book. There are so many modalities: horse therapy, massage, acupuncture, shaman healer, journaling, yoga, athletics of any kind, etc. Some people cook, I don't love to cook, others paint.

My podcast interviews people who have had tragedy and how they are healing. "My message is 'There is a way'." I don't know what your way is, I don't know what anyone's way is. That's the deal. Some weeks I want to go walk on the beach, and that's all I want to do. I just want to walk by myself on the beach and pick up shells. Other weeks I want to go to the gym, and then sometimes I'm ready to ride a horse again. It's all about feeling where you need to be and knowing that you can be in a healing process. That's so important if you realize you are stuck. Do you need professional care? Do you need medication; do you just need a different group of friends? Do you have toxic people around you? Do you need to get toxic people away from you? "My message is… we can all be on a healing path, in a healing journey, and we have to keep finding what that is at any given time."

Aside from your core message, is there another mantra or saying that you find yourself living by?

Don't be afraid to fail. My dad used to tell me that when I was young. I've always lived by that. I lived by that when I first started working in the corporate world; I lived by it when I was the captain of the cheerleading squad at the University of Oklahoma. Just go for it.

I teach that to Lukas, just don't be afraid to fail. If you don't try, you won't succeed. You won't fail, but you won't succeed either.

It's something we've heard most of our entire lives or have seen in some way or another. It really does speak volumes. You mentioned wanting to become an astronaut, and I picture that old school banner that was above chalkboards, the 'shoot for the moon' in elementary school classrooms.

This journey has taught you and so many others so much, but what do you think is next for you? Where do you see Mindy?

I did not know I was going to open up a software company. My business partner, Lisa Cooper, and I joined forces for Workplace Healing. We are going to change corporate culture. We are going to help corporations reintegrate their employees, their team members, who have had life tragedies, who have experienced a death of a loved one, a divorce or are in the middle of caregiving. Everyone experiences life disruptions and then we have to go back to work. We have to make a living. When we're trying to do that and there's so much chaos going on in our home life, we need normalcy at our workspace. We're hoping that is a place of normal or we have control in that space. However, when our company leadership does not know what to do for us or say to us during our turmoil and grief, they might choose to stay quiet. We might begin to feel our chaos from homelife sneaking into our workplace. There is a need for training our corporate leadership about the importance of providing empathy alongside work related conversations when their employee is grieving. Over half of US employees will consider leaving their employer if they are not acknowledged during a grieving period. Our Human Recovery Plan™ software platform provides an innovative, thorough, and simple solution to put in the hands of a leader, manager, or supervisor to increase their confidence in communicating with a grieving team member. The manager/supervisor is the 'Plan Builder,' and they build the plan for their team member/employee. The plan is personalized with head and heart-based tactics which will be offered in conversation and/or actions from the company to the team member/employee.

Ultimately, a corporation wants their employees to stay employed. To make it back from the grief and chaos. A company does need return on investment to survive, let alone succeed. Our Human Recovery Plan™ software platform offers head and heart-based tactics to address what is missing, the balance of head and heart in our workplaces.

They just don't know how.

They are trying to igure out the balance and don't want to be crass. They don't want to push you, but also need to know if you are ready to return. Our software gives them verbiage to say, the timeline of when to say them, and we give them ideas of what to do both head and heart based. Our innovative approach is that if you allocate 50% to head and 50% to heart, and you offer the employee this when they come back on board, you're going to tether that employee back to you and you're going to help them. You're going to help them heal, your company heal, and help your team be a better team while teaching empathy. You are going to exercise your empathy muscle. This is where I'm going to be; in workplace healing and helping people build the Human Recovery Plan™ software platform.

This sounds like a game changer; you know that, right?

I'm super excited about it.

Final question for you. What if?

What if Dad and Reat were never murdered? Where would I be? I have no idea. Everything in my life has changed since April 13, everything. I still am married to the same man, that hasn't changed. But that's been a struggle for both of us. We love each other just so much to the core and we need one another, but it is still so hard. I am in a different location, I am in a different state, I've been in different jobs, I've done so many different things that I had no idea I would ever do. What if?

Mindy, today's the 13th...

It's the 13th...

STORY LAUNCHER

TURNING THE PAGES

Meet Ondi Laure: best-selling author and owner of Story Launcher Publishing.

Don't mess with this cowgirl! She may put pen to paper for a living, but she can also wrangle a herd of cattle in a moment's notice.

When Ondi Laure isn't producing best-selling books or coaching authors into careers, she can be found on horseback, roaming the lands of infamous outlaws near her ranch in Wyoming.

Her passion for writing began at a young age, and her ancestral lineage would prove she would do so. As Ondi shares her story of strength, survival, and changing the world, we ask you, what were you born to do?

△ △ △

CK: Ondi, you, and I both know that this project has been two years in the making and to have you in my corner has meant the world. You've taught me so much in the last couple of years about the author space and in helping me live out a childhood dream. More importantly, what was your childhood dream?

OL: *Thank you, Callie. You have taught me just as much as I've taught you. So, thank you from the bottom of my heart.*

My childhood dream was to write. Growing up I wasn't a reader as a kid. I didn't have my nose buried in the books. I always had a pen in my hand and was always fanatical about fancy pens, fancy notebooks, and fancy paper. I wouldn't read. I would sit up in the hills near my home and I would write stories. I would hide in my closet and write poems and songs. It's been my life's plan and my life's mission to write books and stories.

CK: How did you first become an author? What did that process look like for you?

OL: *I became an author in the fourth grade. My grandmother was a huge inspiration. She was an author and wrote her life story about her parents, grandparents, and the reservation. Her grandfather was also an author and was highly educated. I just knew in my heart of hearts that that is what I wanted to do. I remember sitting on my kitchen floor apartment in college with my mom, trying to decide a direction to go in. I had taken a lot of science classes and knew I wanted to write, but never thought of it as a career.*

I was told growing up that that was 'artsy fartsy' and you could never pay the bills as an author, that you needed to do something you could make money at. So, I entertained the idea of becoming a geologist. I liked rocks and had always been a rockhound collecting. I could do that and write in my spare time for fun. Again, I was advised by an adult that told me I wouldn't be able to pay the bills as a geologist. It was horrible advice! So, I got my nursing degree and didn't stay in the field very long because it got in the way of my writing. 12-hour shifts weren't conducive to burning midnight oil and writing stories.

In the meantime, I had married a rancher and was spending time in agriculture, which would have been the perfect environment for a writer; however, I was married to a tough man.

Raising my babies and being a mother was my sole job.

My writing wasn't approved upon, so I kept it a secret. I was very shunned and belittled, made to feel very yucky that I liked to write and was an artist.

I hid it and repressed it for years. The first book I published in 2004, I actually wrote at night on the bathroom floor so he wouldn't see me writing. It was such a fight.

It became such a struggle in my own home if I was caught writing. You would think I was caught doing drugs or something really bad. That was the beginning of me breaking out of that shell, out of that cage I had put myself in. In all reality, I really put myself there, Callie. Because I allowed it and hadn't established personal boundaries and been confident in who I was. To stand up for myself against my spouse and say, this is who I am! You can't take this away from me. I didn't know that then. Hindsight is 20/20.

CK: When you had your first book published, what did that look like for you? You had been secretly writing and hiding that gift, how were you able to get that gift out into the world and share the message?

I was elated and so excited. That was really when I stood up for myself. I had got it traditionally published. It was a middle-grade fiction children's book, so it wasn't a big book. It was a cowboy book. We've always been told, write what you know! I knew the cowboy stuff! (I've come a long way!) LAUGHS.

There are two sides to this coin; this was really a turning point for me. I'm capable and talented, and I have this gift. I was elated because I was doing the very thing I wanted most. I wanted to scream, 'IN YOUR FACE, I'LL HOLD MY PEN!' It was a 'watch me now' moment. However, the flip side of that coin was how do I do this?

I was published by a traditional house and realized I was opening another can of worms. All the marketing, publicity, and getting yourself out there was going to push me out of my comfort zone. I had been a ranch wife for 20 years. I wasn't ready to do lives on Facebook, interviews, or book signings. I was dipping my toe into other waters, learning how to come out of my shell and treating myself to this new potential. It has been a long haul. In fact, it's been 12 years coming from that point to where I am today.

Do you feel like writing helped you heal in a sense?

Absolutely. It not only helped me heal, but it also helped me survive those years. Those years of being under someone's thumb and being in an abusive relationship, not physically, but verbally and mentally. If I hadn't had my writing, if I hadn't had my pens and paper (they were not fancy by any stretch), and if I hadn't had that outlet and craft, I wouldn't be here today. It really saved me and helped me through those days.

Wow. Thank you for sharing that story of survival because that's what it was.

I am so elated, even though that doesn't even begin to express the language of elation, to have overcome all of that and have the gift I have to help others really hone in on their own. To show them what they are capable of, it's unsurmountable.

I can't even fathom what you've gone through emotionally. What I do know is that it took courage and bravery. This book talks about the inner grit, and that's exactly what you have.

Yes. And tenacity. As long as we don't give up. Anybody can accomplish greatness. We can live into our highest versions of ourselves and the possibilities the universe holds for us, GOD's universe, or whoever your higher source is. We all have that capacity and ability if we just don't give up and we just keep in the game. Some days, it's hard to get one foot in front of the other, but as long as we're taking steps forward every day, baby steps even, we're still in the game and that tenacity to stay in the game is crucial.

> "As long as we don't give up. Anybody can accomplish greatness."
> — Ondi Laure

Absolutely. After you broke free and had published your first book, how did you continue to expand your career from there? What happened next?

There were a lot of dark days after that. It took another five years to really break free, and I had to completely reinvent myself and my identity. The marriage had been going south for years and we divorced. Then, I found myself running a ranch and there was very little time to write. There was a lot of emotional baggage and having a broken home while I was raising young children.

Only in the last six years am I now just coming all the way through it. In 2017, my ex-husband committed suicide. That was horrific in itself. I was free and out of the ridicule and shame, however, my kids were still surrounded by it because they had to spend time with him. I was having to support them and be both the advocate for them through that time, and that was challenging.

So, in the last six years, the healing had just begun. I continued to journal; journaling is the number one savior of everything. We talk about this in the writing group that you are a part of Callie. It's the gratitude. If we can think of all the things we are grateful for and just focus on our gratitude, it raises our vibration, raises our frequency, and it begins to change not only how we are on the inside, but how we see the world on the outside. Even on the days when the only thing you have to be grateful for is your cup of hot tea or a roof over your head, you're still holding yourself in a space and that frequency of gratitude.

Take this a few steps forward. For example, when we are just learning and taking those baby steps, there is gratitude in that. We can be grateful for things that have yet to happen or are to come. There are things I know that I want and hold close to my heart. I already know how it feels, even before they are realized, and I'm grateful for it. This may sound hokey, but it works. It's magic.

Incredible. Your words give me hope, and yet, I can't help but think of those who aren't there yet emotionally and mentally. What would you tell somebody that is aching on the inside and is ready to find that light?

The first thing I would tell people is to keep your dreams and take really good care of them, be very careful who you share them with. There are a lot of naysayers, even people that love us or we are really close to. For some reason, they want to keep you in their sphere; there are a lot of reasons, but maybe they are afraid to lose us? They'll put our dreams down and take the wind out of our sails, so just be very, very careful of who you share your dreams with and your greatness with. Until you are so firm and confident in your own beliefs and power, then share it. You will know when you've reached that point where you are confident enough to share it; until then it's sacred.

That reminds me of the saying, 'keep your head down and your heels in the ground.'

I was just visiting with someone about that! In Australia, they have the Tall Poppy Syndrome; if your head stands out, it gets chopped. Our whole lives we've been taught to play small, to not make a lot of noise, to not exceed beyond the standard, etc.

And I don't mean to contradict what I just said. Once you're confident in your stance, your belief, skill sets, then by all means shout it from the rooftops and be that Tall Poppy! Until you have the confidence and that grit, don't do it. Work on yourself, your inner dialogue, your inner beliefs, affirmations, your gratitude journal; work on all of that on the inside. Once you're ready, shout it loud and shout it every day!

Which is exactly what this book is about. It's about building up that inner grit and that inner fight to the naysayers and the ones that told you no, to the ones that tried to stop you. All of the collaborators in this book, including myself, have run into that. I'm personally one of those people that if you tell me 'No' while pushing down a dream of mine, I'm more willing to come back with an inner fight and tell you to watch me now.

Hell yeah! That's a great incentive. It's a super, super motivator when people do that. That's a magnificent asset to have, Callie. I didn't have that asset until now. It took me a long time to build that up and I just didn't have that. I would hear things like that and take it to heart.

I remember after I had written the first book, I was so excited about all the stories I had written, and my ex-husband said something to me that I will never forget; it changed my life. He said, 'You're never going to change the world; you can't change the world. What is it that you are going to change?' He continued to say it. That was the motivator I needed, and that is why I'm changing the world one book at a time.

You once told our writing group that 'books change people and people change the world.'

Now, here you are as the owner of your own company, having written behind the curtain, and now the world knows your name. Your pieces have helped change and inspire people. How many books have you written to date?

I have written eight books and published three. It takes time! Currently, I am writing two more, so I've written a dozen overall.

What has been your favorite book that you have written or had published?

My favorite one is the one I'm writing now. It's a non-fiction memoir about the journey of a storyteller. I'm the storyteller and am sharing my journey in how I became an author. It's the toughest book I've ever written because it's closest to my heart. My other favorite book is part of a trilogy I am writing now. Sophia is the feminine version of Christ, and her books were parts of the Bible written by Mary Magdalene. Those are probably the most important books I will write. Morningstar is the first part of that trilogy, which I just recently took off Amazon because I'm changing the marketing. I want to market this to a young adult versus adult. I believe that we all have a book of a lifetime in us that we need to produce, and the Morningstar trilogy is mine.

You are a publisher now and have your own publishing house. When did you decide, you were going to help authors with their own journeys rather than it being vice versa?

Story Launcher Publishing is the name of my company and our writer's coaching program, Aligned Writing Method. I created it when I started to launch my second novel. The flip side of writing a book is how to market and get the book distributed, all the business aspects. A traditional publishing company will take 80-90+ percent of book royalties. In this day and age, the author is doing the bulk of work for marketing and is responsible for doing 80-95% of its entirety, if not more. I think my first couple of books I received 14%. I maybe made two dollars a book. It was ridiculous. I thought, that's not fair and it's not right. We have birthed these books, they are going to transform, not only our lives, but our readers as well. Why should we be giving away all our royalties?

Today, the book industry is HUGE, and anyone is able to write a book. Even if you self-publish, Amazon is keeping 35-70% of royalties off Kindle editions, if not more. There's an unnecessary evil in some regard with Amazon; however, the author deserves to keep all their royalties. We shouldn't be relying on publishing companies, publicists, and media to keep it. They don't deserve a stake in our game that we've invented and really created. It's so important that authors, both fiction and nonfiction, have the knowledge and tools to keep what they have created. That's priceless. It's knowing how to play the game and what steps to take. You shouldn't have to pay somebody for the life of your story when you can do it yourself. It does take work and incentive, but it's knowing the ropes and hoops to jump through to be able to make things happen successfully.

In 2014, I was offered a contract for Morningstar. (That book alone took me a decade to write because I was learning so many assets at the time.) The publishing house wasn't going to give me an advance, however, there was a $4K advance to fly somewhere for an interview. But they were going to keep 86% of my royalties, so I turned it down. I was going to do it myself. Shortly after, I started helping others publish their books and found joy in that, so here we are today.

What would you tell a first-time author that is looking to write a book or has written a book and wants to get it distributed? What does that process look like for them?

The first thing I would tell them is to treat your book like a business. A book is a business, and the first thing you need is a mission statement. Write a mission statement around your book. Everybody has heard that a book is a business card on steroids. That's true in some regard, but it's more than a business card. It's a brand and it's you.

That's the first step. The second thing I encourage people to do is know your WHY. What is your purpose in writing a book? As you know, writing a book is not an easy task and is not for the faint of heart. There's going to be times where you want to curl up with the dogs under your desk. There's a lot of self-talk and there's going to be dark days.

If you're writing a book to get more leads, fine. Why do you need more leads? To make more money. So, you have to know these whys before you begin. Whatever your 'why' is, put it in a picture frame so you see that every day. That 'why' is going to pick you up and drag you back up to the table. It's going to see you through, knowing why you're doing this in the first place.

What is your WHY?

My WHY is to change the world because I was told I couldn't. Every book that I get out there, every book that I help publish, or even write, is changing somebody's world for the better. Those are the only books I work with, that I write, and that are here to make the world a better place.

It's the WATCH ME NOW.

That's the motivator. I have to thank my ex-husband because he gave me that tenacity after all was said and done.

Some of the hardest times in our lives have also taught us some of the biggest lessons. I think back to when I was working in my last corporate job before stepping into entrepreneurship. I was working for a nasty individual, and the day I got let go was one of the biggest lessons I could have taught myself. It brought out something in me and enough to say that I will never let somebody do that to me again. Now, as an entrepreneur, you can get fired in a sense from helping people, but I was no longer going to let a corporation decide my destiny. That was my experience.

So many authors have become entrepreneurs. What is your definition of a female entrepreneur?

My definition of a female entrepreneur is a woman who has taken charge. Not only of her future, but her now. She is no longer accepting nos from the naysayers. She is creating a life that she deserves and demands.

That was a great definition. What's next for you? What is next for your business, Story Launcher Publishing, and where do you see it all going?

Currently, we are growing our Aligned Writing Method program for writers and we are in conversation to launch a new partnership for authors who are ready to launch their books and receive the publicity they deserve!

My gift is in book production. I would like to bring in more coaches that are better at certain tasks than I am. For example, Callie, you're really good at the money part of things and helping others find sponsors for their books. That is such a unique avenue and amazing asset of our program. So, I'm wanting to bring in more authors that can help in that regard.

Everyone says you don't buy a book by its cover, but we do. It's just human nature. We gravitate to book covers that entice us and make us curious. I'm not a graphic designer, so I'm always looking for talented designers and editorial work. I'm really good at the developmental edits for both fiction and non; that's part of the process that I love. I'm not great at copy and line editing; that's not my cup of tea. So really bringing in people and team players that thrive in areas and excel in their greatness. Let them shine where they are good.

You know when to delegate to others' genius zones.

Absolutely. For example, I had a gal working with me over the last couple of years, and I was giving her odds and ends jobs to do. She wasn't really picking up the stuff that I was laying down. Even though I wanted her to, she really excelled in online/social media. I just happened to catch that and realized she needed to be doing that! I gave her a new role and she was thriving there!

My focus point is to really get authors through the program and onto the next phases. I have a couple gals just starting at ground zero, and some that we have been working with for some time. I really want to streamline it more. Not to hurry the authors, but to support them and get them to the next stage in a more reasonable time frame.

Over the last couple of years, my own writing has fallen on the back burner because I've been so busy in the business. I need to write; I know that about myself. My advice for any entrepreneur is know where you get replenished, where you need to go and fill your cup. As an entrepreneur, we give so much and are very service oriented. So, know where you need to go to fill your cup. I'm really carving out my sacred writing time space to finish my next books. It's easier to say you're writing a book, then to actually sit your butt in the chair is a whole other ballgame. I really have to practice what I preach and make room for that. Otherwise, there won't be a Story Launcher.

Writing is so sacred to you, but what else recharges you? How does Ondi recharge between being an entrepreneur, running the ranch, and being a publisher? How do you carve out that extra space?

You just have to take it. Yesterday, I went for a ski. We had four inches of fresh powder and I just put on my shoes! You have to be a little selfish. My daughter wanted me to come help her with her 4H steer and I told her, 'You got it! He's halter broke now, you can handle it, I'm going skiing.' Of course, I invited her to go...

Thatta way, Momma!

Being selfish isn't always a bad thing. Even for 20-30 minutes, you have to be.

That's something I'm still learning to do for myself and have a hard time doing. You are right when you're talking about giving. We can give, give, give all day, even when you're working on your own material. It's still about giving and placing it out there for others.

Yes, and boundaries. We don't learn so much about boundaries in school, but it's something I wish I had known. I'm getting better at setting boundaries in what I'm willing to put in for clients and even in our home as a family. Once we set boundaries, know where you want to be, where you're going, and build around that.

I like that your intentions are around healthy boundaries. Because boundaries can be misconstrued and used negatively, and I think there are a lot of miscon-ceptions about what boundaries mean. Over the last couple of years, I have seen others be very manipulative with setting boundaries. It becomes ego-based and not about what it should be. It's not about telling somebody to not do XYZ; that's control and ego. However, you can control how you respond and react, what you're willing to and not willing to draw the line in the sand on.

Yes! Boundaries will get tested constantly. It's easier to set a boundary than to fix one. I'll give you two examples; the first one is setting a healthy boundary. For my own health and vitality, I gave up drinking coffee this past year. I used to be a pot a day kinda gal, however, it was a lot easier than I thought it would be; I gave it up cold turkey. My husband is not much of a coffee drinker, however, my stepson moved in with us and he is a coffee drinker. This is a small, simple boundary, but I am not responsible for getting up in the morning and making a pot of coffee for him. I don't do it. A part of me was tempted to, and then I thought, no, because then it will become an expectation. It's the same with cooking meals every night. I love to cook, but it's not my duty or expectation. Last night I asked what was for dinner? My stepson cooked us hamburgers. That is an example of showing it's not all on me to cook every meal, and easily established now that he's living with us.

I also have had to reassess this expectation from my mother, who I love dearly and with all my heart, that wants me to call her first thing every morning. I have done that my entire life. In the past six months, I have tried to reestablish this expectation and boundary that I'm busy in the mornings getting a kid off to school, feeding cows, and don't have the time. It's not that I don't love my mom, but I've got a full start and can call her when I have time to talk and can visit. I'll admit, it's not an easy one. That healthy boundary wasn't established by me years ago and I've been eating the crows since. I think a lot of us have those boundaries with our mothers!

As individuals, we change as we grow and evolve as we gain more personal intellect. What do you think is the biggest way in which you have grown?

Definitely my confidence. I've always been fairly confident, but nothing like I thought I would be now. I had confidence as a young adult, but I lost a lot of that in my early marriage and have since gained it back. I used to be a mountaineer before I got married! I was a guide, climbing The Wind River mountains with people, so I was very confident.

But where have I changed the most? That's a tough one. I guess knowing that anything I put my mind to, I can accomplish. We are all capable of anything and everything we put our minds to. Our hearts as well, more than our minds. There's nothing in this world that can stop us.

It is such a powerful statement, yet that statement alone can be hard for so many to act on because we do have fear and find ourselves up against many roadblocks. You mentioned once having the confidence, then lost a part of yourself in that life chapter, but then found it again.

What if you wouldn't have found that confidence? Today, you have confidence and so much more! So, if I were to ask you this final question, 'What if?' How would you finish the sentence?

I would still be writing on the bathroom floor at night. I would still be stuck. I would be a very unhealthy individual. And all the people that I've influenced and have been helping wouldn't be.

Now you don't have to anymore.

No.

BEYOND THE SIDELINES

Your life IS the Super Bowl Championship game. It doesn't matter how many losses or wins it took for you to get here, because you get to control the narrative. You don't have to walk off the field, never to return again, after a heartbreaking loss. You get to walk off the field with your head held high knowing you gave it your all. And, even at times if it doesn't feel as if you've "won" the game, you have to know that you did. You've taken more wins home than you can even recall. Because not everyone tries. Not everyone has the courage to go for the winning touchdown when all the odds are stacked against them. And, by now you know there are A LOT of odds. You get to declare the difference between telling yourself you can have it all or are you just simply not allowing it? The only thing standing between you and your opponent is the scoreboard. It's that simple.

To all of you that are about to turn the last page of this book, I encourage you to make this promise to yourselves: I WILL NO LONGER CONTINUE TO WATCH FROM THE SIDELINES. Say it out loud. Now, SAY IT AGAIN!

Friends, you are UN-RE-LENT-ING. There is an inner fight in all of you that no one can take away. And, whether you knew it or not, it's also one of the reasons you picked up this book.

Let me ask you this: if someone turned the pages of your playbook, what would they see? Did you go for the big plays, or did you play a game that we've already watched time and time again? What is the legacy you want to leave behind?

I'M GIVING YOU THE OPPORTUNITY TO SHARE WITH THE WORLD WHO YOU WERE MADE TO BE!

Just because this is the last page of this book does not mean the game is over. This is just the beginning of a new wave for entrepreneurship in our respective industries. If there is one thing, I have learned over the last two years in working on this piece, it is that there are so many more stories to be shared and heard, including yours.

Are you ready to become a featured author in 2024? Do you know someone that has a sink or swim story? Let us know!

Come Sweat or Silt Vol. 2 is taking applicants for those who are ready to play at the next level!

We want to hear from:
The UNSTOPPABLE leaders
Who are a testament to their rising foundations + empires.
Who have fallen trap to the 'smoke and mirrors' of empty promises.
Are on a mission to create exponential growth.
Are no longer willing to just 'survive.'
Luxury Businesses
Celebrity Magnetizers
Shark Tank Business Owners
Elite Icons
and counting…

Because if not now, when? No matter if you are in:

- Coaching/Consulting
- 6 to 7-Figure Retreat Masterminds
- Media

- Investing
- Luxe Partnerships OR
- Brand Elevation + Product deals…

YOU HAVE A STORY THAT IS WAITING ON THE OTHER SIDE

I know, without a doubt, this book was written for so much more than just me. This book already had a place on bookshelves throughout the country; I just had to make the choice to get it here. I can only begin to contemplate the ways this book has coached you, and I know it has the potential to help:

- Create ICONIC partnerships.
- Create red carpet launches and events.
- Embrace life's curveballs!
- Show you how to plan for the biggest PR show of your life!
- What you were born to do while living on this Mother Freaking Earth!
- Explain the myth buster of one size fits all! You do you, boo.

If any of these lights a spark within you, it's time. Our lives are like filling the pages of a book from cover-to-cover, sharing the stories of our memories and lifetime achievements. It is my hope that, with this beautifully published and successful piece of work, we all continue to fill the pages. We leave pieces of our legacy for the ones that dream after us, so that we can write our own rules, and inspire others to follow.

In the words of our timeless matriarch, Coco Chanel….

"DON'T BE LIKE THE REST OF THEM DARLING."

APPLY HERE:
sweatorsilt.com

ACKNOWLEDGMENTS

This is what it must feel like when an Academy/Oscar/Emmy-award winner steps up to accept the coveted award of a lifetime. A much-anticipated finale in a high-achievement year, only to dissipate as a new category and a new winner takes your place.

Except, as a writer, my words of credit and acceptance go beyond the preservation of 45 seconds, as the cue of music that signifies my time in the spotlight is over, doesn't exist here.

Don't get me wrong, there is music playing! And I am here raising my glass of champagne to all of you!

Without you, there wouldn't be this piece of work. That as this book came to fruition, I realized was a sounding board for leading entrepreneurs who are making waves in their industries. That these women, who have dug themselves out of the trenches, building their own brand of personal grit along the way, DECIDED. Having embraced life, its lessons and hardships, continued to go up against all the naysayers because they BELIEVED in themselves enough to say, "WATCH ME NOW."

I still remember the day I DECIDED. Not only for myself, but for all of you. There was this fire that was lit inside of me. Why wasn't anyone telling the real, raw truth of what this journey truly takes? Why wasn't this out there already?! Was anyone else tired of being played and pitched the smoke and mirrors act? Enough already!

Every single individual I have chosen to be a part of this piece or my journey in writing this book over the last two years was hand-selected for a reason! If you know me well enough, you know that I go straight to the top and I NEVER settle!

I make it a point to align myself with individuals that seek a higher purpose, believe in miracles, dream BIG and take the required action to make it happen.

To Ondi Laure Culver and the Story Launcher Publishing Team, this book would not be in the hands of many without all your efforts! You all have been open to my suggestions and creative insight since day one! You allowed me to run this path and go for it in ways I had not envisioned! Ondi, this has been one helluva ride with you and I cannot wait to see what we do next! Oh, the places we will go with this book alone!

To Liz Kampschroeder, we have been training for life for over a decade now. You have watched me climb my mountain and have helped me realize that there is limitless potential in summiting my goals! Your mentorship and friendship are such a gift!

A Special Thanks to all the collaborators who believed in this project, who said YES in speaking the truth and sharing their messages: Jodie Rodenbaugh, Amber McCue, Nat Tolhopf, Julie Moe, Eve Overland, Cara Clark, Melissa Moore, Melinda Dunn, Mindy Corporon, Kelly Pascuzzi and Ryann Dowdy. Cheers to all of our Champagne Dreams!

To my husband, Warren, we have set out on this journey together. One where we have chosen each other and get to create what is possible. I love you. Maliyah and Elayna (my bonus daughters), whatever you go through in life, don't let it stop you in becoming who you are meant to be. You get to choose to hold your head high regardless of circumstances.

To my family and extended family, thank you for being excited as I took these steps in sharing my gift to the world. We have shared so many memories, ones that I hold close to my heart, and for the ones we will continue to create! For our angels in heaven, we think about you every day and I will always carry you with me.

Lastly, to all of you who will take this book across the world, THANK YOU! This is absolutely a dream come true and just the start of another chapter in my life! I rolled the dice and bet on myself…will you do the same?

With abundance,

REDEFINING YOUR RESOURCES

AMBER MCCUE:
Instagram: @ambermccue
Partner with Amber McCue to grow your business:
ambermccue.com/programs

RYANN DOWDY:
Instagram: @RyannDowdyOfficial
TikTok: @RyannDowdyOfficial
Facebook: *https://www.facebook.com/groups/beintheroom*

CARA CLARK:
Instagram: @CaraClarkNutrition
Web site: caraclarknutrition.com

KELLY PASCUZZI:
Instagram: @kellypascuzzi
Web site: CLnow.com
Facebook: *https://www.facebook.com/kelly.pascuzzi.5*

MELINDA DUNN:
Instagram: @gloss_rx_
Web site: glossrxkc.com

JULIE MOE:
Instagram: @zoobymedia
Twitter: @IAmJulieMoe
Web site: zoobymedia.com

CALLIE KATZ:
For media inquiries, please contact:
powerhausepartnerships@gmail.com
Book Tour + Signings:
Instagram: @sweatorsilt

EVE OVERLAND:
Instagram: @eveoverlandfitness
Web site: eveoverlandfitness.com
Download the fit52 App: fit52.com

NAT TOLHOPF:
Instagram: @natalie_tolhopf_business_coach
YouTube: https://www.youtube.com/channel/UCHTFvNtPS83KxNenKsJOe0g
LinkedIn: https://www.linkedin.com/in/natalietolhopf/
Facebook: https://www.facebook.com/NatalieTolhopfSellwithConfidence
Web site: natalietolhopf.com

MELISSA MOORE:
Instagram: @melissa_g_moore

JODIE RODENBAUGH:
Instagram: @jodierodenbaugh
Facebook: Join our Raising Love Genius movement: www.facebook.com/groups/RaisingLoveGenius/
Web site: jodierodenbaugh.com

MINDY CORPORON:
Instagram: @mindycorporon
Web site(s):
mindycorporon.com
Foundation: givesevendays.org
Workplacehealing.com

ONDI LAURE CULVER:
Instagram: @storylauncher
Facebook: Free Writing Group:
www.facebook.com/groups/storylauncher
Story Launcher Publishing: storylauncher.com

www.ingramcontent.com/pod-product-compliance
Lightning Source LLC
Chambersburg PA
CBHW051803100526
44592CB00016B/2543